MORTGAGE RIP-OFFS: Learn the Secret to Saving Thousands Before You Apply

by
Pat Mazor

Table of Contents

DEDICATION

This book is dedicated to Linda Joyce, who taught me the intricacies of mortgage and commercial lending; my mother who taught me how to write; my father who taught me the importance of caring; my children who taught me how to love; my wonderful friend Sara Loewen who inspired me to grow; and of course Georgene Harkness, for turning a collection of words into a published book. I am truly blessed and grateful to have these people in my life.

FOREWORD

We hear a lot about the national debt but not so much about personal debt anymore. Americans are in debt up to their eyeballs. Right now, in a country of about 313 million people over 610 million credit cards have been issued. That's almost two for every child and adult. The average family has about $16,000 in credit card debt. However, credit card debt pales when compared to mortgage debt in the United States. In early 2012, the total mortgage debt on one- to four-family houses totaled about $10.2 trillion; that's $10,200,000,000,000.

I have a house for sale. It's a nice three bedroom, two bath starter home in a nice neighborhood and it has been appraised at $100,000. I'll be glad to sell it to you for only $194,724. Sounds like a bad deal doesn't it? One you are not likely to take. But if you just purchased a $100,000 home with a 5.125%, 30-year mortgage you just agreed to pay $194,723.64 for that nice little $100,000 home. Could you have done better? In most cases the answer is *yes*.

Most people spend a lot of time shopping around for the best deal on their credit cards. After all, we want the frequent flier miles, the rewards program, the cash back percentage and the low introductory interest rate. We expend all that effort on selecting the best credit cards for our average family credit card debt of $16,000. Why not spend the same effort in making the really big decision, the one that might have you paying $194,724 for a $100,000 home?

In *Mortgage Rip-Offs,* Pat Mazor leads you through what is wrong with the real estate/mortgage industry. If you haven't figured it out, there is a big conflict of interest problem. The people *working* for you, the real estate agent, appraiser, and mortgage loan officer, are really working for themselves at your expense. It is in your best interest to minimize your costs, the price of your home and your interest rate. It is in their best interest to maximize your costs because their commissions are computed based on what you pay. The more you pay, the more they make.

Have you ever noticed that some salespeople like to throw jargon and acronyms around. Knowledge is power. If you don't know exactly what is being explained to you and what everything means, and most importantly, its effect on your pocket book, then you are a mark, a target to be taken advantage of. In Chapter Five, Pat walks you through the mortgage jargon. After you read this chapter you will know what CLTV, LTV, MI, PMI, HELOC and much more are, the reasons you should care about them, how the mortgage loan application process works, and how to reduce your costs.

As I age, my eyes get worse and so I don't like fine print. Nevertheless I *always* read the fine print on contracts, and a loan is a contract. Chapter Thirteen discusses disclosures ranging from the Good Faith Estimate (the most important of the disclosures), the TIL (truth in lending disclosure, or how much is your new home really going to cost), and a whole slew of other disclosures. While you don't need to understand all of the disclosures in detail, you do need to understand the Good Faith Estimate and the TIL. Make sure that your Originator explains all of that to you, ask relevant questions, and never sign on the dotted line until you know exactly what you are signing. This chapter summarizes all of the common disclosures so that you can enter closing prepared.

Chapter One leads you through the submission, processing and underwriting activities that get you successfully to closing. As a Borrower you don't have much to do in this stage of mortgage loan processing but it's nice to know where your loan application is and what is happening to it. After all, it feels really good to call a loan officer and ask, "Is my file stacked and ready for underwriting?" After you read this chapter, you will know what my question means.

Everyone says that you should lock in your interest rate while rates are low. What does that really mean? Can it really save you money? Can it save you enough money so that it is worth doing? Locking in a 5.000%, 30 year mortgage when it looks like rates are headed to 5.375% can save you almost $10,000 on a $100,000 mortgage. Pat explains why and when to lock interest rates, and when not to do it as well.

Most of the chapters in this book are a little technical, not too technical, but they are about numbers and processes. Pat mentions a key point a few times. Originators are salespeople and salespeople tend to think that your money is their money. Keep this in mind when working with a mortgage company.

I wish that Pat would have written this book before I purchased my first home. I was young, right out of college with an accounting degree and an MBA and I thought that I knew it all. I didn't. College didn't prepare me for buying a home and as a result I made some bad decisions and in retrospect paid more in fees and interest than I should have. Learn from my mistakes: read the book first, before you apply.

Dr. David S. Murphy, CPA, CFS, PhD
The Fraud Doc

INTRODUCTION

The first manuscript for this book was written in 2007 just as the foreclosure crisis got underway. Little did anyone realize that it would continue for another five years. Now, in 2013, housing prices are still at their lowest in decades as are mortgage loan interest rates. As of January 2013, purchases are finally starting to show activity again while mortgage rates remain steady with little volatility. With over five years of foreclosures, there is a huge inventory of homes on the market and pricing has shown only moderate increases, especially in those markets that were hit hardest by the crisis. In other words, now is certainly the right time to be considering investing in a home. The first key to success is to remember the primary rule when buying a home: location, location, location. It isn't just a house. It is your home. The second key is preparation and that's what this book is all about - saving money through preparation.

Unfortunately, the people and businesses most responsible for the foreclosure crisis are still in the mortgage industry and, if what is seen in the news and on the internet is any indication, little has changed in terms of mentality or sense of responsibility toward borrowers.

The idea, in writing this, is to help you understand the industry and how it works. More than that, it is to help you "beat the system" or at least make it work in your favor. After reading this book and working through the recommended action steps, you will be armed with a knowledge of 1) the difference between a mortgage broker and a direct lender; 2) how mortgage companies (brokers) are compensated and how you can use that knowledge to your advantage; 3) how to negotiate for lower fees and a lower interest rate (which means lower monthly payments); 4) how to fill out the loan application properly and completely; and 5) how to pre-assemble a complete loan application package.

What does this do for you? First, it will save time. You will be completely prepared to apply for a mortgage before you ever talk to a loan originator. Second, when you understand how the system works, you are in a position to negotiate for lower upfront fees and a lower interest rate, which translates into two things. The first is a lower payment. The second is lower total out-of-pocket expense over the life of the loan. A savings of even 1/8th of a point (0.125%) can mean a great deal over the course of 360 payments – the life of a 30 year mortgage.

Finally, when you have worked through all the action steps in this book, you will have a complete loan application package ready for submission. That saves time and lots of it. There are "**slow-down points**" in both processing and underwriting that are identified throughout the book. You can beat those **slow-down points**.

Throughout the book, I refer to sample documents and forms that can be found on the web. In some cases, I include references to sample documents. In most cases you will want to be able to read what is here in the book while looking at those sample forms and documents or while completing the Loan Application Form. If you would like the forms and sample documents, please feel free to send me an email or visit my website to request the forms and sample documents. The email address is Pat@PatMazor.com and the website is www.PatMazor.com.

CHAPTER 1: WHO IS WHO

The purpose of this opening chapter is to introduce you to the people who will be involved in the submission, processing, and underwriting of your loan file and, at the same time, the process itself.

For the most part, you will be dealing with a loan officer or loan originator. Those two terms are interchangeable in a sense. From 2002 to 2007, when I was a loan officer, that was the term given to someone who worked up a mortgage loan application and file. With the devastation of the foreclosure crisis, banks attempted to distance themselves from mortgage broker companies and the revised regulations now require the term "Originator" rather than "Officer." Unfortunately, the general public has no idea what the differences are.

The Loan Originator: This is the person you will interact with most. He or she will help you complete the mortgage loan application and provide you with a list of the documents you'll need to submit for the processing and underwriting of your loan. Once the application has been approved, he'll tell you the rate that is available that day and ask if you want to "lock in" the rate and proceed to closing.

The one thing most people do not understand about the Originator is that he or she is, almost always, paid commission. Where that comes from will be explained in detail in Chapter 4: Compensation.

The Mortgage Broker/Mortgage Company: This is the person the Originator works for. You may or may not meet the Broker. Brokers rarely get involved in loan applications and transactions unless there is a problem. This person, however, will be the one who communicates with the Lender or Investor when it comes time to lock the rate and proceed to closing. Any deviations from usual practices, i.e., requests for reduced upfront fees, a lower rate than what is offered to the customer, or an unusual request like, "I understand that you need to be fairly compensated for your work but I want to have input in that," will go right to the Broker. Seldom does an Originator have the authority to make those decisions.

The Processor: The Processor is a person who may work full time for the broker or may be an independent contractor who works for many brokers. She will review the file with an eye toward making sure that it is complete in every way and ready for submission to the Lender. In addition, she will request multiple Verifications that demonstrate the information entered in the application is accurate. When the file is complete, it will be "stacked" and forwarded to the Lender or Investor for underwriting. It is common for a Borrower to speak with a Processor about his file and missing items. The alternative is for the Processor to call the Originator, who then calls the Borrower, who then brings needed documentation to the Originator, who then forwards it to the Processor. Consider the amount of time lost with that approach. However, many Originators do not want customers talking to the Processor for whatever reason – control, fear of the Processor recommending a different company, or other reasons.

The Lender: Taking one example, Bank of America (in the trade, "BofA") is a Lender and Servicer who is sometimes the Investor. Let me break that down a bit. Bank of America is both a wholesale lender and a direct lender. In other words, BofA will offer its mortgage loan products directly through its banks but also offer those same, or similar, products to Brokers on a wholesale level. Where can you get the better deal? Believe it or not, through a Broker. Why? Because the Broker has flexibility that BofA's mortgage loan officers don't have. The day you want to lock your rate with BofA directly, you will be told what rate is available. There will be no room for negotiation. The upfront fees may be the same, lower, or higher. However, again, there will be little or no room for negotiation. It is always a good idea, during the early shopping phase, to contact a direct lender as well as mortgage brokers. In Chapter 11: Finding the Right Mortgage Company, there will be a list of key questions to ask any company that you interview, whether broker or direct lender. *Keep this one rule in mind at all times. You are the customer. It's your money. It's your decision.*

The Servicer: In a typical conventional loan, the Lender and Servicer are the same company. Using Bank of America as the example, after your mortgage loan has closed, you will make your payments to BofA. The company to whom you make your payments is the Servicer. That company is servicing your loan. They do this by accepting and processing your payments, retaining a percentage for handling, sending money to the Investor, the homeowner's insurance company, and retaining money for paying the County Assessor when property taxes come due.

If you have owned a home before, you may have received a notice that your loan was sold to another bank. The loan was not sold. The servicing was sold. In early 2007, a great many lenders went out of business and loans were "sold" to banks that were still in business. For anyone who owned a home between 2006 and 2011, there is a good probability that at least one such notice was received. At no time, however, did the Investor change.

The Investor: This is the entity with the money that will be invested so you can buy or refinance your home. You know the Investors best by the names Fannie Mae and Freddie Mac. Simply put, people invest in mortgage-related bonds and mutual funds. That investment capital goes to Freddie or Fannie and then goes to the banks that offer mortgage products. The bank services the mortgage loan, retaining a percentage of the proceeds. The balance of your payment ultimately goes to the Investor. All too often, you will hear an Originator use the term "Investor" meaning the "Lender" which will become the "Servicer." The Investor is the financial entity that ultimately makes the investment of capital that funds your mortgage. Freddie and Fannie only invest in conventional loans. For non-conventional loans (greater than Freddie and Fannie's lending limits), the loan may be funded by a bank, although this is rare. More often, they are funded through major investment portfolios. The Investor will not be involved in your mortgage loan until it has closed and been funded. Likewise, you will never make your payments to the Investor.

The Underwriter: This person works for the Lender/Servicer much like the Processor works for a Broker or Direct Lender. The Underwriter is the person who makes the final decision as to whether to approve the loan. Only the Underwriter can use the word "Approval." In other words, there is no such thing as a "Pre-Approval." If you hear the word "Pre-Approval," from an Originator, that is a red flag because Originators do not have the authority to use the word "approval." The Underwriter goes over the entire file, which has been stacked in the order required by that Lender, and verifies that everything is accurate. Providing the file meets the Lender's criteria, the Underwriter issues an approval and a "clear to close" meaning the closing can be scheduled.

The Process: The process begins with you completing a mortgage loan application. Once that has been properly and completely filled out, the Originator will obtain a copy of your credit report. The industry term is, "pull your credit." He will make his initial determination based on the application and credit report.

If he believes there is a good potential for approval by an Underwriter, he will submit your file electronically to a Lender appropriate for your mortgage application. He should, at this point, provide you a number of disclosures. There are two to look over. The first is the Good Faith Estimate. The second is the Truth-in-Lending Statement.

Provided the Originator received a positive response from the Lender (it's not an Approval), you will be given a shopping list of documents to provide with your application and credit report. This is the first *slow-down point* in the transaction because it will take you time to assemble the required documents. Unless, of course, you have already prepared those documents.

Once you have the required documents, you will provide those to the Originator who gives them to the Processor so she can assemble your file. Here is the next *slow-down point*. The Processor usually has between five and 30 files that she is working on at the same time. Typically, a Processor will review all her files once each day looking for next steps. One of the key points at this stage is called Verifications. A properly completed application will include the information needed for those. However, most Originators skip that part, leaving it to the Processor. And now there are two *slow-down points*. The Processor or Originator will call, asking for the information needed to obtain the Verifications. That information will then be used to generate the Verification forms and mail those to your bank, landlord, employer, and others. Once you have read this book and worked the action steps, you will eliminate all of the **slow-down points** mentioned thus far.

Once the Processor has everything she needs, she will "stack" the file and transmit it to the Lender – usually by Priority Mail (a minor *slow-down point*). Smart Brokers send submission files by overnight post, but that adds to their cost. Most Brokers are big into income and not real big into outgo. A typical stacking order is: 1) Loan Submission Cover Sheet (much like a Mortgage Loan Summary; see Chapter 11), 2) Loan Application (the 1003), 3) Credit Report, 4) Purchase Contract (purchase) or most recent HUD-1 Settlement

Statement (refinance), 5) Verifications, 6) Letters of Explanation, 7) Bank Statements, 8) Payroll Statements, 9) Homeowners Insurance documentation, 10) Appraisal, 11) Survey, 12) Other Documentation.

Now the file is in front of the Underwriter – the decision-maker – and is gone over in very close detail. The Underwriter will issue a "Conditions" letter to the Broker and Originator. The Conditions are typically for things that are missing which creates a **slow-down point**. The other possibility will be for updated information, usually bank statements or payroll check stubs. These must be current.

Let me interject something here. What if, before you ever talked to the Originator, you had all the required documentation assembled and organized? How much time would be saved? And, what if you knew that between the time your file was given to the Originator and received by the Underwriter, another pay period would elapse or another bank statement would be made available. Would you plan to provide those? Of course you would. But what if, like most people applying for a mortgage, you didn't know about this? Do you see how knowing this can save you time?

This is going to cause a hiccup in the system. Originators and Processors are not accustomed to Borrowers who are prepared.

Once all the conditions are satisfied, the Underwriter issues a "Clear to Close" and you are free to schedule your closing. However, you don't have the rate for your loan yet. The Originator will call you and say something along the lines of, "Okay, we have a clear to close and need to lock your rate. I can get you 4 and 3/4th (4.750%) today." If you agree to that, the Broker sends in a Lock Rate Notice to the Lender and your closing will be scheduled with the title company.

That's the process in a nutshell.

CHAPTER 2: THE LOAN OFFICER

In 2002, I entered the mortgage lending profession. For the previous seven years, I had owned and operated a successful aviation consulting firm. Then came 9/11 and the company's two foundational clients – who produced 70% of the revenue – ceased operations. 9/11 and the failure of my business had seriously taken the wind out of my sails.

One Friday night, a friend was over for dinner. He asked how things were going. When I told him, he said, "Hey, you're a good salesman. Why don't you come to work for me doing refinance mortgages? Best of all, you'll make a lot of money." Knowing I needed a change, I jumped in with both feet.

Three days later, I was at my desk ready to go to work. L, my friend and boss, explained that my job was to answer the telephone, take an application (which was illegal since I wasn't licensed), tell customers to send in an application fee of $300, and we'd be happy to take care of their mortgage.

Within a few days, I learned that the company offered some of the absolute lowest rates available in the market. Having been in sales and business for 30 years, I made what I considered to be some natural assumptions. Either there were volume discounts involved or L had found a resource that was way ahead of everyone else. The logic versus the reality would not hit for another few weeks.

During this neophyte period, I became quite adept at discussing all that I understood about the mortgage process. I had the chance to observe L posting his rates on the internet. And I also observed that he would adjust costs and other things to reduce the Annual Percentage Rate (APR) – not to be confused with the Note Rate. The APR is based on the Note Rate (4.50%, 4.75%, etc.) plus any costs involved with the loan, i.e., closing costs. So, if a mortgage broker reduces the appraisal fee from $350.00 to $250.00, this will reduce the APR. Two points: First of all, it is up to the appraiser to determine the appraisal fee, not the mortgage company. Second, and this was the important lesson, the APR influenced positioning on the internet. The lower the APR, the higher the ranking on the websites.

Of course, I immediately took the classes necessary to become licensed, took the test, and passed. At this point, I was licensed and allowed to discuss mortgages top to bottom. Being a quick study, I caught on to the laws, rules, regulations, and intricacies of mortgage lending fairly quickly. Shortly after I received my license, two of my loans closed and I received about $6,000. In the meantime, I had been giving the same basic sales pitch (since I was a salesman) to everyone who called in, "Well, we have excellent lenders and get preferred rates because of our high volume. We are more competitive than other companies because we keep our costs as low as possible. We are very aggressive in the marketplace." It was all a lie.

About the sixth week into the job, I had 15 loans in the "pipeline." The pipeline is the industry word for the number of loans an originator has in process. In all likelihood, I was looking at about $30,000 in commissions. Nearly everyone I spoke with sent in their $300.00. It was on my third loan that I ran into trouble.

L had instructed me that morning to call a Borrower and tell him we could lock his loan at 5.375% (5 and 3/8th). This was during the "Refi Craze" and rates were volatile. The Borrower said he'd call me back. He did early that afternoon and said, "On the internet, it says your rate today is 5.125% - a quarter point difference. What's the deal?" Well, I didn't know what the deal was so I said I'd ask my manager and call him back. That evening, I began to put all the pieces of the puzzle together. We were advertising a "par rate" – where the company would not make a dime. That was the 5.125%. We would have Borrowers send in $300.00 application fees and hook them because they didn't want to lose their $300.00 and didn't understand that they were going to lose much more than that in the end.

Then, when we were ready to lock the rate and prepare to close the loan, we would give them the real rate where we got yield spread premium – commission of between 0.75% and 1.50%. So, the real rate, the one we **sold** to our customers was 1/4 point (0.250%) higher than what was advertised. In other words, it was "bait and switch."

I didn't sleep very well that night. I had to think it all over.

Having sold for over 20 years, and having held myself to a high standard, I was in a dilemma. So, I decided to quit. I went in the next morning. L and the other loan officer, B, were both there and I told them about the conversation with my borrower. They said, "Well, just tell him it's a different program." I said, "But it's not a different program; same lender, same program. We're lying." It took five rounds of this discussion, "different program" then me "no, we're lying," before they would admit that the whole thing was a scam. In other words, lying was okay with them. They could rationalize it all out.

I walked away. I walked away from L and his company. I walked away from 15 loans. I walked away from $30,000 in commissions. All because I wouldn't do business that way.

Out of Mortgage Company No. 1, into Mortgage Company No. 2. Linda Joyce and her company, First Mortgage Solutions. Linda became my mentor. A whole new world opened up to me. I began focusing on construction loans. Construction loans are very complex. Most mortgage loan officers focused on refinance loans. For me, construction lending meant more challenge and less competition. I traveled all over Florida talking to people who were building custom homes. Specialization paid off.

A builder called. He had two custom homes that were nearly complete and ready for sale. The builder wanted to buy some land that was on the ocean. The price of the land was $10,000,000. The sales prices for the two existing houses were in the $8,000,000 range. The sale price for the two houses to be constructed were $25,000,000 and $35,000,000. I had entered the world of commercial lending. Linda took me by the hand and walked me through the entire process from creating a construction loan summary to a complete proposal for a bank. She helped me prepare to meet with the bank's lending committee and to show how the two existing homes, the property, and the two homes to be built could be packaged in a single cross-collateralized loan thereby benefiting the builder, the bank, and buyers.

Linda taught me how to structure this $70,000,000 deal. Linda Joyce was the exact opposite of what I had seen before. She taught me how to be a pro at mortgage lending.

Then, in 2005, I moved to Texas, re-polished my resume, took out the yellow pages, made a list of the mortgage companies in town, and went out banging on doors. At this point, the score was 1 to 1. I had been with one good mortgage company, and one bad mortgage company. So – I had a 50/50 chance for another good one, right? Wrong. Mortgage Company No. 3 – subprime sweatshop. The owner/manager, E, explained that they focused on the subprime market, that most of their customers were first time homebuyers, and that my job was to take an application, pull the credit report, and submit both to their three top Lenders. After the first couple customers, and taking a hard look at what I was seeing, my reaction was, "Are you joking? Who is going to fund a mortgage with these folks?" Well, there **_were_** companies who would do that. In the first eight months of 2007, most went out of business never to be seen again.

Here was E's deal: three on the front, two on the back. In other words, the fees were 3% (origination, mortgage broker, application, other) and closing costs (the front) and a 2% yield spread premium commission (the back). This increased the Borrowers' rate by at least 1%. The rates were already very high at 10% to 11% - getting a 2% commission put an additional 1% or more on the rate. Even worse, the programs were adjustable rate mortgages. The logic? The customers would have to come back in two or three years and refinance.

This company preyed (predatory lending) on people's ignorance. Were they in compliance? They went way overboard to make sure everything was in compliance – right down to doing disclosures (as required by RESPA) on the spot. Way ahead of the three day rule that says any applicant for a mortgage must receive a full set of disclosures within three days of submitting the application. As to ethics and consideration of consequences, that was another story altogether.

After a few weeks, I walked into E's office and said, "E – logically speaking, about 80% of these folks are headed for foreclosure. They are right on the line in terms of their budget and their credit history is iffy. All in all, these are not going to be good loans." E's response, "Why do you care?" Because I did care. I saw a catastrophe in the making that the lenders and investors seemed to miss. Of course, as we all know now, my prediction was right on the mark. As a side note, E's company went out of business in 2009. However, I recently saw that they are back specializing in Reverse Mortgages – now preying on seniors.

I was faced with another dilemma. Luckily, another door I knocked on belonged to one of the then Big 5 (now Big 3). Just as I was trying to decide how to resolve my conflict, I was called in for interviews. And then I was hired. Three mortgage companies thus far – the score: 1 good, 2 bad.

Potentially, any major direct lender would be an excellent company.

With this company, I had the freedom to attempt to do what I had done before – create my own unique market. Having been in wholesale/distribution selling, I drew a circle 100 miles around where I lived and said, "This is my territory." Then, I created a four-week call schedule and hit the road. This was how I found my market – or maybe it found me.

In my first round, a real estate agent had a borrower contact me. The borrower had some challenges but an FHA loan was possible. So, I called on the customer. During our discussion, he said, "They are going to build 300 new homes here in the next five years." To a construction lending specialist, that is music to the ears. Thus, I began to focus on this area and was fortunate enough to meet a pretty decent real estate agent, D. For the first few months, I officed out of my car. Then D said, "Hey, why don't you come over here – I'll give you an office to use if you'll help my customers." Deal.

D is completely West Texas in personality to my Western Washington. But our ethics and attitude toward business are similar. She would come to me with loans under $50,000 and ask if I'd work them up. Why? Because nobody wanted loan amounts that low – couldn't make enough money. So, of course I would do them for her when I could.

The area had three unique cultures. And my market grew from one of them. Call it intuition, gut feeling, whatever. I hit it off with that market. The people are very sophisticated in terms of money but not in terms of paperwork. Since I tend to explain everything thoroughly, maybe that's the reason we got along so well.

At this time, the company was going through some changes in management and attitude. The biggest challenge faced by the local branches was processing and underwriting. The problem, it seemed, is that nobody wanted to identify the problem: being short-staffed. Without an adequate number of processors and underwriters, loans do not get closed. I had tons of fallout (loans that just died because borrowers lost patience) and went elsewhere.

D, bless her heart, said to me, "You know? I have this company in Dallas I sometimes work with – they are really smart, you are really smart, you would be a good match." Enter Company No. 5. The score? 2 bad, 1 good, 1 neutral. When I spoke with EL, the company's managing director, his first words to me were, "You are going to make a lot of money." I'd heard that before. Something at the back of my mind said, "This is a red flag."

Then I remembered: I would make a lot of money gouging customers. I lasted one month. The score: 3 bad, 1 good, 1 neutral.

Then came No. 6 and the branch manager, F. I had jumped out of the frying pan a couple months earlier and kept ending up in hotter fires. With No. 6, I had latitude concerning the amount of money I wanted to make on loans, meaning I could treat customers fairly. They were being submitted, processed, and moved along – but at a snail's pace. And then, the bottom fell out. Eight months into the foreclosure crisis, the industry finally caught up with reality. The subprime market died. Unfortunately, another area died as well.

The industry threw out the baby with the bath water. Clearly, the problem was not really the subprime market and lending money to people who weren't qualified. The problem was stated income loans. A stated income loan is where the applicant says, "I earn this amount of money each year," even though they can't prove it. But, they have excellent credit scores. Does it make sense to take people's words on this? Sometimes yes. Sometimes no. So, the industry being reactive in nature, responded with, "All the time 'no.'"

My primary market was made up of people who were self-employed. They, being savvy with money, write off every expense they can on their income tax returns. There is only one small problem – that means the income that shows when all is said and done is minimal, and generally not enough to qualify for a mortgage. Baby and bath water. No self-employed stated income loans.

The score: 4 bad, 1 good, 1 neutral. The point of all this? I believe that there are few mortgage companies with integrity out there. I believed that in 2007. Sadly, I believe that today in 2013. Why? Because the system, and here is the disease, promotes situations that put originators in a middle-ground, conflict of interest position. They can only earn a good living by raising the interest rates on people's mortgages.

Needless to say, this will attract people who are dishonest and greedy. In my opinion, the subprime market, adjustable rate mortgages, foreclosures, and all the rest are merely symptoms – not the disease. The disease is the system itself.

CHAPTER 3: MORTGAGE TYPES and AMORTIZATION

There are five types of mortgages today. Two are common: Purchase and Refinance. Two are a little less common: Construction and Construction-to-Permanent. There is the fifth one, a relative newcomer: the Reverse Mortgage.

Second, there are different types of Amortization – how the interest is calculated, adjusted, and applied to the Mortgage Loan. They are: Fixed Rate, Adjustable or Variable Rate, Interest Only, and Graduated Payment Mortgage.

A Purchase Mortgage Loan is for buying and financing a home. A Refinance Mortgage Loan is for creating a new loan on your current home. Construction loans are for construction of a new home. The Construction-to-Permanent programs are for building a new home or rehabilitating an existing property with a mortgage tied in once the construction is completed.

The Reverse Mortgage

The Reverse Mortgage is, in my opinion, a bad idea. A family has lived in a home for 20 or more years and gained equity – the home is worth more than they owe. The Reverse Mortgage becomes a monthly payment to the homeowners with the interest and principal now accruing (in reverse) against the property. One of the things that indicates this is a bad idea to me is the fact that the sub-prime specialists (who contributed a great deal to the foreclosure crisis) are now in the reverse mortgage business. I am not a financial planner nor investment consultant. I would, however, recommend talking to one of these professionals before entering into a reverse mortgage transaction.

The Purchase

In a purchase transaction, there are three elements: (a) the sales price, (b) the amount of down payment, and (c) the appraised value of the home.   If the sellers are asking $100,000 and you, as the buyer and borrower, are willing to put $10,000 (10%) down on the home, then logically the loan-to-value ratio would be 90%.

As long as the house appraises for more than $100,000, the loan-to-value ratio stays at 90%. If, however, the appraised value comes in at $95,000 – $5,000 under the sales price – then the loan-to-value ratio is calculated using the $90,000 loan amount and the $95,000 appraised value – which creates a loan-to-value ratio of 94.7% ($95,000 ÷ $100,000).

There is a second loan-to-value ratio called "combined loan-to-value" or CLTV. This comes into play with combination loan programs, including seller-carried second mortgages. A combination loan is two loans in one program. Perhaps you have heard phrases like 80/20, 80/15/5, 80/10/10. An 80/20 is two loans – an 80% primary mortgage with a 20% second mortgage "piggy-backed" onto the primary.   Using the $100,000 purchase price example, the LTV with the primary loan is 80% ($80,000). The LTV with the second mortgage is 20% ($20,000). The combined loan-to-value ratio is 100% - the 80% plus the 20%. An 80/15/5 is the same idea with the second mortgage being 15% or $15,000 in this case, with a 5% down payment. The LTVs are 80% and 15%, with a CLTV of 95%.   The 80/10/10 is an 80% first mortgage, a 10% second mortgage, and a 10% down payment – the CLTV is 90%.

Why would someone opt for a combination program?   To eliminate the mortgage insurance or, to put in the jargon, the

MI or PMI. What is MI? It is an insurance policy that you, the borrower, pay for. The purpose? To insure against default. If the borrower fails to make the payments, and the home goes into foreclosure (default), then the insurance company that covers the mortgage (with mortgage insurance) helps to recover the costs of the loss and protect the investor. FHA loans (and FHA is an insurance provider, **not** a lender) always require mortgage insurance premiums for a minimum of five years. Usually, with the exception of FHA, mortgage insurance goes away when the loan amount is 80% or less of the value of the home. One of the ongoing scams is to tell borrowers, "Oh listen, if the value of your home goes up to the point that you only owe 80% or less, then you can refinance your home and eliminate the mortgage insurance." Do you know what it really takes? An appraisal. It takes an appraisal that shows that the house is worth enough so that whatever is owed against it is 80% or less than the appraised value.

The concept, and it probably was pretty solid at one time, is that when a person owes more than 80% of the value on a house, they are less committed to keeping the house. Or, to put it the other way, once they have paid for 20% or more on their house, they won't let the investment go easily. Does that always hold true? Sadly, no it doesn't.

In any event, the combination concept was designed to put the monthly payment difference (because the second mortgage is at a much higher rate) in the lender's and investor's pockets rather than an insurance company's.

The Refinance

Anyone who owned a home prior to 2002 has probably been through the refinance process. Rates bottomed out late 2002 through early 2004, and have now bottomed out again. Where mortgage money was readily available in 2004, it is not today. Homeowners who had an interest rate of 7% or higher refinanced in order to reduce their monthly payment. Smart move. There is good news and bad news here for both the lenders and the homeowners.

Lenders first. They were making 7% or higher in terms of return – that got cut to a little over 5%. That's the bad news. Ah, but the good news. The mortgage starts over again – the initial three to seven years of payments are almost all interest. There's the good news. For the homeowners, the good news is the lower payment. The bad news is that it starts all over again and all they are paying is interest for those first few years.

I figured out when it makes sense to refinance by printing out an amortization schedule and discovered that to refinance from a 7% mortgage to a 5.25% mortgage (as an example), it takes about seven years to make up the difference between the lower payments, the initial interest payments, and the closing costs. Being a responsible loan officer, this became one of my qualifying questions: How long do you plan to keep the house? If the answer is less than seven years, you will lose money. If more than seven years, you'll make up the difference.

I remember the first time I did the math and went through the scenario with a borrower over the phone. As soon as I had completed the call, L immediately said, "Don't tell them that." This leads to a question. If I, as a Originator, know that the borrower is going to lose money with the transaction, and I go forward with the loan anyway, am I committing an act of predatory lending? According to the regulations, no. According to real life, in my opinion, yes.

The rules concerning LTV, CLTV, mortgage insurance, combination loans, and all the rest are the same with refinance mortgage loans. However, there are other considerations. First, there are two types of refinance programs: rate and term, and cash-out.

Rate and term refi's (reef-eye – "refi" is short for refinance) were what was common in 2003-2004. "Rate and term" is jargon for "reduce the rate, change the term." People lowered their rates but changed their term from whatever they had left on the existing mortgage (let's say 25 years as an example) to 30. These programs are still popular. More so, considering the number of adjustable rate mortgages that were created between 2004 and 2007 that have since adjusted - the rate going up 2% or more. An 8% loan is now 11%; a 10% loan is now 13%. The rate goes up. The payment goes up.

However, there is the other type of refinance program – the cash-out. With these, people are borrowing against the equity in their home and taking cash. This can be used for home improvements, debt consolidation, and other things. This is a full refinance program meaning the clock starts ticking all over again. The amount that can be borrowed varies from 80% to 100%. At one time, in 2005, there were a couple of states that allowed people to borrow up to 135% of the value of their home. Remember my comments about the mortgage industry being short-sighted? This is an excellent example of that.

Additionally, there are sometimes dollar amount limits. For example, in some states, a borrower cannot take more than $100,000, no matter how much equity they have. The purpose behind these state regulations is plain. The goal is to make sure that people do not end up owing more than the house is worth, commonly called "being upside-down."

Let's consider a real life example – Southeast Florida. Between 2002 and 2005, property values doubled. Some homeowners leveraged (borrowed money) in cash-out refinance and home equity lines of credit (in essence, a second or third mortgage). So, a person buys a home in 2002 for $210,000. In 2004, the home is worth (according to market value) $400,000. Why not borrow $100,000 against the home using an equity line to start a business, buy a rental property, or whatever? They can. Let's say the primary mortgage is for

$200,000, and there is a $100,000 obligation in a HELOC (pronounced Hee-lock - - Home Equity Line of Credit). The value of the home in 2005 is $400,000. Thus, the combined loan-to-value ratio (CLTV) is 75%. What happens if the market crashes – which it did. Now the house is worth $200,000 again, but there is $300,000 owing against it. That makes the CLTV 150%.

In other words, the borrower now owes considerably more than the property is worth or is likely to be worth again in the near future. As I said, this is called being "upside down" in a property, a serious problem. A HELOC is a simplified cash-out refinance. It is a second mortgage. There are some major risks involved. All HELOCs are adjustable – usually based on the Prime Rate. The example I just provided is for a real home, a home I owned at one time. I knew the buyer/borrower. Last month, I was told that the home went into foreclosure.

Foreclosures have been at an all-time high for seven years as of 2013. This then reduces property values. Housing is like any other industry: supply and demand. Foreclosures increase the supply while lowering the overall value of the market.

One final item on refinance mortgage loans: did you see those ads on the internet that said something along the lines of "Refinance Your $250,000 Mortgage - $524.00 per month." Anyone in their right mind would immediately say, "How can they do that?" Well, let me tell you. It's called an interest-only loan. It has a start term of one, three, or six months. The rate is very attractive. In 2003, the rate was a low-to-mid 1%. In 2007, they were in the low 3s. Wow, that sounds great, doesn't it?

Point Number One: INTEREST ONLY. You are not paying down the principal at all.

Point Number Two: IT'S AN ADJUSTABLE – these programs don't come with a fixed option.

Point Number Three: These first one to six payments do not cover the real interest payment, and the difference is being added to the principal balance of the loan. This is called negative amortization.

Point Number Four: The lender is going to make the money back – absolutely guaranteed. Bait and switch? No, because those programs are available and legitimate. But, the toe is on the line.

Construction Loans

Construction loans are complex, challenging, and fun – at least they were for me. They are very challenging in terms of documentation. At the same time, people are building their dream home. There is a lot of excitement, lots of planning, and fun.

Up until a few years ago, it took two loans to build a home and obtain a mortgage.

The first was called the interim or construction loan. These loans facilitate the construction of the house. The borrowers only have to cover the interest payments – usually the rate is based on the Prime Rate plus 1%. Once the house was finished, the customers secured a mortgage and that was that. One problem with this method is that it requires two closings and two sets of closing costs. The other bigger problem is changes in the customers' lives – loss of job, health problems, deteriorating credit, and other things. So the people borrowed money to build the house, but now can't qualify for a mortgage. The bank that did the construction loan ends up with the house. Not good for the bank. Not good for the borrowers. Not good for anyone.

Additionally, often the builder's final draw (where he has all the profit) is held back awaiting the resale of the house. In these situations, there are no winners – only losers.

Construction-to-Permanent

The One-Time Close or Construction-to-Permanent loan program is one loan, not two. One set of closing costs, not two. One program with a seamless transition from the construction phase (called interim financing) to the mortgage. A large number of lenders offered these programs with numerous variations. However, they were complex – very complex. Lots and lots of paperwork, and three levels of qualification: borrowers, builder, project. And all three have to measure up. The borrowers had to qualify both in terms of credit history and assets/liabilities. Now keep in mind, most of these people already have a home. They are going to have to live in that home until the new house is finished. Supporting two homes can and does create problems.

The builder is reviewed. This can be something simple like references from customers, subcontractors, and vendors, or it can be complex – the lender wants to see tax returns and financial statements. Finally, the project: does the planned home make sense financially? Are the costs in line with the projected value upon completion? A typical good example would be for a lot purchased for $15,000 and holding its value. The construction costs are $150,000 so the total project costs are $165,000. Provided the builder doesn't go over, the end value will be $165,000.

Like I said, there is a lot of paperwork, but the challenge of making it all happen can be very rewarding. In mortgage lending, this was my specialty.

Construction lending also encompasses additional projects like demolition and rebuild, rehabilitation loans, and buy and rehabilitate loans. Demolition and rebuild (commonly called demo/rebuild) is literally that. Someone really likes a piece of property. I mean they really like it. They are going to buy the house (and the property of course), destroy the house, and build a new house there. A little heads-up is necessary here. The sellers are not just selling the property and the house doesn't count. The price is for both.

The property (without a house) only has so much value. A new house is going to be built but it only has so much value. In nearly every case, the buyers are going to have to come up with some serious money to offset the difference between the out-of-pocket costs and the final value. Here is a real example: property with current home: $500,000. Value of property without a home: $100,000. New home construction costs and value: $650,000. Property plus new home: $750,000. But the cost is $1,150,000. The borrowers will have to pay the $450,000 difference. In some cases, the demolition is for a house that needs destruction. Unfortunately, even though this was the original intention, it is seldom the case. The party buying the property will be required to come up with the difference in cash – after all, the land and new home will not appraise for the value of the costs: land, original home, demolition, and new home.

Rehabilitation loans take an existing property and home with the idea of rebuilding it or doing some major improvement or expansion. Otherwise, these are quite similar to standard construction to permanent programs.

Amortization

There are four options in terms of amortization. Amortization is how the interest is calculated: (a) fixed rate: the rate is the same throughout the life of the loan, (b) ARM (Adjustable Rate Mortgage, also known as a variable rate): the rate will adjust or vary over time consistent with the movement of financial markets, (c) GPM (Graduated Payment Mortgage): the payments increase for a specific period of time and then level off, and (d) the infamous Other. Remember the comments about "Interest Only" programs? That's one of the "Other" options. Interest only, adjustable rate, and graduated payment amortization schedules can, and many times do, create what is known as negative amortization. Negative amortization happens when, instead of reducing the principal balance, the principal balance increases from unpaid interest. Under these programs, because the "teaser rate/interest only" payment is not sufficient to cover all of the interest due for that month, the amount of interest that is left is added to the principal. Instead of seeing the principal balance go down each month, it goes up. The "hook" is the "low payment." The problem is that low payments cost a great deal more than nearly any borrower will realize.

How is it that I call these programs "real life" predatory lending? Think about it for a second. The originator knows that the rate and payments are going to increase. The originator is hoping and planning on "selling" the borrower a refinance mortgage in two, three or five years, depending on the initial start rate term. Seldom, however, does an originator tell the borrower these things. In fact, the vast majority of originators gloss over these very important details. Thus, real life predatory lending.

Let me cover Adjustable/Variable Rate Mortgages. Adjustable rate mortgages are called 2/28, 3/27, 5/25, 7/23, 9/21, etc. The first number indicates the number of years for the "start rate." When you agree to an adjustable rate mortgage, the rate you are given is for that initial two, three, or more years. After that, the rate changes. Some originators will ignore the cyclical nature of interest rates and say, "Heck, your rate may actually go down." That is not likely to happen. With the 5/25, the rate you are quoted, that you lock in, will be the interest rate for the first five years of the mortgage. After that, it adjusts – the reason these are called adjustable rate mortgages.

What about principal-only payments? In that small West Texas community where I built a market, the majority of the people there work to pay off their homes as quickly as possible. They do this with "principal only" additional payments. Most of the people are self-employed – ranchers and farmers. When the harvest comes in, or a herd sells, or a project is completed, they take a portion of their profits and pay extra money against the mortgage. This doesn't reduce the payment, but it can shorten the term considerably. In fact, I did some research and found that the majority of people in the market I served paid off their homes completely within seven years of the original purchase. Interesting. These folks understood the value of owning their homes free and clear.

Specialty Programs – SIVA and SISA

The first specialty program is the Stated Income, Verified Assets (SIVA) (pronounced "See-vah"), which is a program where the borrowers are stating, but not having to document their income, but will document their assets. This program is still available. There are two "no documentation" programs. The second is a SISA (pronounced "Siss-Ah") – Stated Income, Stated Asset. Nothing has to be documented. This is not available any longer. There **was** a third program - the NINA (pronounced "Nee-Nah") NO Income NO Assets. I can hear a collective groan and someone asking, "Wait a minute. Are you telling me that someone can apply for a mortgage loan with no income and no assets?" Not anymore.

There was always a "hit" for SIVA, SISA, and NINA programs. A "hit" means a higher interest rate. In some cases, it is a little hit – 0.125% to 0.375%. In other cases, it is a big hit – upwards of 3.000%. It all depends on the factors involved.

CHAPTER 4: COMPENSATION

To begin, I am going to ask you to recognize that the Loan Originator is a commissioned salesperson. He may have sold other things before getting into the mortgage industry. He is used to "taking control of the sales process." That is to his advantage and to your disadvantage. If you pick the right company, you will work <u>together with</u> the Loan Originator to reach the end result: a mortgage you are as pleased with as much as you are with the home you are buying. Until you know that the Originator is someone you can work <u>with</u>, it is better to maintain control of the relationship.

As I just said, the majority of Mortgage Loan Originators are paid straight-commission. In other words, if they don't sell, they don't eat. This is information that you can use to your advantage. The Originator earns a percentage, usually half, of whatever the Broker/Company earns from mortgages they originate.

So where does the revenue come from? Two places: Upfront fees, and Yield Spread Premium/Back-End Commission. The Good Faith Estimate I worked with back in 2007 was easier to understand than the document used today. In some ways, the new form is better. However, it is far more difficult for someone unfamiliar with Good Faith Estimates to understand than the older version. Likewise, although it is covered in this version, the commission (back-end fee) is no longer identified as Yield Spread Premium – even though it still is that. The Mortgage Company sells you a higher interest rate and gets a percentage of the increase in the return the Lender will realize from your increased payments.

You can Google "sample good faith estimate 2012" and see numerous examples. The GFE (Good Faith Estimate) I was reviewing and found to be most helpful was located at: www.oaktreefunding.com.

The "Summary of your loan" section is a great addition, especially the check boxes related to "Can your interest rate rise?" Specifically, that section addresses variable or adjustable rate mortgages (a really bad idea right now), interest only loans, and other things that can have a negative impact on the mortgage.

At the bottom of page 1, you see "Your Adjusted Origination Charges." These are the upfront fees charged by the Mortgage Company. If you are reviewing the same sample I am, this looks pretty good at this point. The Broker (Mortgage Company and Broker mean the same thing) looks to only be charging $995.00 to the Borrower. Let's move on.

At the top of Page 2, it says that actual Origination Charges are $6,477.40 but the Borrower is receiving a credit of $5,482.40 for an interest rate of 4.500%. In other words, the Broker is receiving $5,482.40 in Back-End Commission which is 2.25% of the loan amount of $243,662.00. Using an old rate lock-in sheet that I have, the difference between the percentage of a loan with a 2.25% yield spread and a par rate (no commission to the Broker), is 7/8th of a point or 0.875%. This rate sheet is for rates that are in the 6% range rather than the 4% range. So, I will reduce the adjustment down to 5/8th of a point or 0.625% which would be a rate of 3.875% rather than 4.500%. Let's look at the difference and what that means both in payment and over the life of the loan.

The calculator I'm using can be found at www.mortgagecalculator.org. The principal and interest monthly payment is $1,234.60. And at 3.875% (3 and 7/8th), the payment is $1,145.79, a difference of $88.81. It will take

62 months to pay that $5,482.40 and over the life of the loan, it will cost the Borrower $31,971.60.

Although this new section of the GFE provides more information and much clearer information, it is still not completely open. The first check box allows for all the fees to be paid up front. The second check box which shows the Back-End Commission without calling it that shows how much the Broker intends to earn. The third check box allows for a negotiated lower rate, assuming you will pay those fees upfront. At least the Department of Housing and Urban Development was kind enough to point out which choice increases your closing (settlement) costs and which decreases it. This is far more complete than the previous version.

I have saved this sample Good Faith Estimate. It is included with the free document package I offer to readers through my website www.PatMazor.com.

The point I am making is that both the upfront (Origination) fees and the back-end (Commission) fees are negotiable. So, that means that a question like, "How much does your company anticipate earning on my mortgage in percentage or cash?" would be a very fair question. And then, it should be up to you to decide how those fees will be paid – whether upfront or over the course of the loan. You should carefully consider how much your overall expense is increased by opting for the higher rate and lower closing costs.

There is one final point to consider and that is, "How long do you anticipate owning the house?" Keep in mind that this will, in all likelihood, be the largest investment of your life. Speaking to a financial advisor to weigh all sides may be a good choice.

There is a disclosure document that is available one day before closing called the HUD-1 Settlement Statement. That document details exactly how much is paid out in fees and to whom. Google "sample HUD-1 Settlement Statement PDF." The sample I reference and offer to readers came from the Olympia Title of Fort Lauderdale, Florida website (www.OlympiaTitle.org). On page 2 of the sample, you'll see "800. ITEMS PAYABLE IN CONNECTION WITH LOAN." These are the fees paid to the Mortgage Company. It is charging a 1.000% origination fee of $2,402.85 (Line 801). In Line 802 (Credit or charge points for the specific interest chosen – the Back-End Commission) shows a second fee of $2,402.85 (1.000%). There is an Appraisal fee of $495.00 and a Credit Report fee of $14.00. There is no Processing fee. Would a mortgage company work up a $240,285 loan for 2.00%? Often.

As you can imagine, most people do not review the HUD-1 in detail until after the closing. This is just one of over 30 pages of disclosures and documents that you will review and sign at the closing. Does it benefit you to understand this one? It absolutely does because this is the most important disclosure of all. It is a very good idea to contact the title company early and request an opportunity to review the HUD-1 as soon as it is available and to take time understanding each item. There are a ton of resources on the web for learning about the HUD. My emphasis is only on the mortgage fees part of that.

CHAPTER 5: THE JARGON

Let's get into the jargon, and here's a little hint: Use the jargon first, **before** the Originator can. Then, watch (if in person) or listen (if on the phone) for reactions. Do not communicate via email. Picking up on non-verbal (body language) behavior and vocal (tone of voice) behavior will provide valuable information. What are you watching for? Discomfort. What are you listening for? Hesitation, and an indication that the person on the other end of the phone is having to think about how to respond.

1003: (Ten-Oh-Three – 10-0-3) – Uniform Residential Loan Application (FNMA "Fannie Mae" Form 1003, also the FHLMC "Freddie Mac" Form 65). The Originator will say, "Well, the first thing we need to do is take a 1003." When you take control of the interview, you will open with, "We have already completed the 10-0-3. We'll share that with you as well as our credit report and a loan summary we have prepared for your review."

APR: APR is the Annual Percentage Rate which is the note rate of your mortgage plus any settlement (closing) costs. Think of it this way – let's say you have a note rate of 5.750% (five and three-quarters points). If all you had was the principal and interest, it would stay at 5.750%. However, there are charges and fees involved – closing costs, the mortgage company's fees, the appraisal, and so on. At the end of the term of the mortgage (usually 30 years), there is principal, interest, and those charges. So, now if you divide out all those charges over the life of the loan, you would come up with a slightly higher rate which is the APR. Let me provide an example. With a loan rate of 4.500% on a $100,000 mortgage, if you add up the payments and divided by the number of months in the term (usually 360 months/30 years), the math will come out at 4.500% interest. The APR takes the principal and interest (the Note Rate) and then adds the other costs and divides that sum by the term. Thus, a 4.500% Note Rate might be a 4.512% APR.

AU/DU/LP: These are acronyms for the mortgage loan computer programs used by Mortgage Companies and Loan Originators. AU is Automated Underwriting. DU is Desktop Underwriting. LP is Loan Prospector, which is related to Fannie Mae and Freddie Mac. These software applications organize all the information into an electronic file that is transmitted to the Lender's computer system from which an initial opinion is generated.

Closing Costs: Many first time homebuyers do not understand that, at the closing, they will have to pay not only the down payment but the closing costs. Part of those closing costs will be fees paid to the mortgage company – the upfront fees, plus the cost of the appraisal, escrow reserves, and other Borrower-related closing costs.

Conditions: There are two – one affects you; one doesn't. They are "Conditions to Close" and "Conditions to Funding." The Underwriter may send a note to the Processor with a request for additional documentation from you or the mortgage company. These are "Conditions to Close." Of course, if you have already assembled everything and all the documentation is current, i.e., most recent bank statements, then there will be very few Conditions to Close. Conditions to Funding are the responsibility of the title company.

DTI: Debt-to-Income Ratios. There are two DTIs – a front-end, or top, DTI and a back-end, or bottom, DTI. The front-end DTI calculates the ratio of projected housing expense to your monthly gross income. The back-end DTI calculates the ratio of your monthly housing expense and credit obligations to the monthly gross income. We'll get into these in detail in the chapter on calculating ratios.

Fannie Mae: Nickname for the Federal National Mortgage Association (FNMA). Fannie is a government-based agency and Investor. 1003 is the form number for the Loan Application.

Freddie Mac: Nickname for the Federal Home Loan Mortgage Corporation (FHLMC). Freddie is the other government based agency and Investor. The form number here – same exact form, look on the bottom of the first page – is Form 65.

GFE: Good Faith Estimate. The term "GFE" is strictly an insider acronym. Customers never call the Good Faith Estimate a GFE. When you say "GFE" as in "We'll want you to work up a GFE for us," the Originator is going to ask, "Were you a Originator at one time?"

Hits: A "hit" results in an increase in your Note Rate. You will hear something along the lines of, "Well now, there's a hit for doing a cash-out refi as opposed to rate and term." Respond with, "How much of a hit?" This will provoke an internal, "Oh – how do they know what a hit is? Now I've got to look it up on today's rate sheet." And then you'll hear, "Well, today, it would be an eighth (or whatever)." Why "today?" Because rates and hits change daily.

HMDA: – Home Mortgage Disclosure Act (pronounced Hum-dah). A section in the 1003 that relates to disclosure of obligations, defaults, and other things that will affect your credit-worthiness when applying for a mortgage.

The "HUD-1": The U.S. Department of Housing and Urban Development (HUD) Settlement Statement. When you talk about origination fees with an Originator, you might hear something like, "Well, it will all be there on the HUD." Yes, it will. When do you get to see the HUD? It must be made available to you 24 hours prior to the closing. I recommend reviewing that as soon as you can. If the HUD isn't consistent with your agreement with the Originator, you have the option of calling the seller, real estate agent or company and Originator and saying, "We're not going through with the closing. The numbers provided with regard to the mortgage company's fees and commission are not what were promised." The Originator can make changes, even if he says he can't. Of course, he's going to have to pay the "lock change fee" and the "documents re-draw fee." The first is a fee paid to the Lender for changing the Note Rate. The second is a fee paid to the Lender for having to regenerate the Loan Documents with the new closing date. If the mortgage company won't, you are faced with a choice. Remember one of the most important rules in business: **There is no deal so good that you can't walk away**. You can save yourself all this grief by warning the Originator early, "As soon as the HUD is available, we are going to review it. If the numbers are not what have been promised, then we will not go through with the closing." One of two extreme things will happen at this point. Either the Originator is going to say to himself, "I really like these folks. They are going to be so easy to work with." Or, there will be some silent profanity.

If the Originator has to make changes, this may delay the closing (by how much will be up to the Lender and Title Company). Probably, although I don't know this for sure, a day or two.

One more thing on the "HUD" and a place it will come up: If you are going to do a Refi (coming up), the Originator is going to ask for a copy of your most recent HUD. If she asks for a copy of your most recent **Settlement Statement**, you might just have a good Originator on your hands. If she asks for a copy of your **HUD**, probably not. Settlement Statement is the right term; HUD is jargon. Of course, you can take control here as well, "We've already gotten out our most recent HUD and will bring that with us."

Lender/Investor: You might hear, "We have a great relationship with a couple of Investors and can get preferable rates." The terms "Lender" and "Investor" are not synonymous. Mortgage companies do not have relationships with Investors. See Chapter One .

Letters of Explanation (LOE): An LOE or Letter of Explanation is provided to the Underwriter to explain the reason there is negative information on the credit report or in the applicant's credit history. A sample is provided in a later chapter.

Locking Your Rate: You will hear something like, "Okay, today, we can lock your rate at 4 and 7/8th. The Originator is telling you that the mortgage company would be happy to "lock your rate," commit you to that percentage and finish up your file. But the question is, "How much back-end commission are they earning by locking you at 4.875%?"

LTV: Loan-to-Value Ratio. We will go over this in the chapter on ratios. Simply put, it is how much you will owe on the house compared to the purchase price or appraised value, whichever is less.

Mid-Scores: You may get a question of, "Well what are your mid-scores?" assuming you don't say, "Our mid-scores are ...." I offer a resource for obtaining a credit report and will go into detail about the three repositories (reporting agencies) in Chapter 8. There are three scores – the one in the middle is the mid-score and that is the one used for calculating credit-worthiness.

Mortgage Insurance (MI/PMI/MIP): MI stands for Mortgage Insurance. PMI stands for Private Mortgage Insurance. MIP is Mortgage Insurance Premium. They are all the same thing. Mortgage Insurance is an insurance policy against your defaulting on the mortgage. If you were to default, there would still be a foreclosure. However, the mortgage insurance company would be obligated to repay the Lender/Servicer and the Investor for any losses. This is nearly always required when the LTV is 80% or higher and is required on all FHA loans, no matter the LTV.

PI: Principal and Interest: the major portion of your monthly payment.

PITI: Principal, Interest, Taxes, and Insurance – the REAL monthly payment plus any mortgage insurance premium.

Points and Percentages: Originators talk in points, not percentages. Simple: 0.125% is 1/8th of a point; 0.250% is 1/4 of a point; 0.375% is 3/8th of a point; 0.500% is 1/2 point; 0.625% is 5/8th of a point; 0.750% is 3/4 of a point; and 0.875% is 7/8th of a point. They are all graduations of 0.125% or 1/8th of a percentage point. So a rate of 4 and 7/8ths is 4.875%. A 1/8th point hit means that the rate on the loan will be 1/8th percentage point (0.125%) higher because it is a cash-out refi as opposed to a straight rate and term using this example.

Prepaids (also called Reserves): When you purchase a home, in most cases, you will have an escrow account that is controlled by the Lender. You can choose to waive the escrows but, of course, there is a hit. The Lender/Servicer assumes responsibility for making your property tax and homeowner's insurance payments from that escrow account. However, in order to do so, there must be money in the account. At the closing, you will pay money into the escrow account to cover those future payments. To be on the safe side, think six months – six months of homeowner's insurance premium payments and one-half of the year's property taxes.

Refi: (pronounced "Reef-eye.") It's short for "Refinance." You can say (and I'll get to the explanation in that section), "Okay, we're looking for a rate and term Refi with just enough cash out to cover the cost of the closing." ASIDE: It's now a cash-out refi – even when it's just a little cash-out as opposed to a rate and term which takes no cash at all. If you can handle the closing costs without the cash out, that may save you on your rate, your payment and interest over the life of the loan.

RESPA: Real Estate Settlement Procedures Act. The intention of RESPA was to protect consumers. It hasn't worked out that way. A mortgage company is required to provide you with disclosures (except for the HUD-1) within three days of receiving the mortgage loan application. However, at that point, since your note rate hasn't been locked in, you don't know what your finance charges will be. The Good Faith Estimate is just that – an estimate. There is nothing binding. RESPA specifies that there can be no consideration between the real estate agent or company, the mortgage company, and the title company – kick-backs. It still goes on. It's done in cash. It's done under the table. But it still goes on. What Congress and HUD (Housing and Urban Development) seem to miss is that it is impossible to regulate integrity.

Seasoning: The length of time the money you are using for the down payment and closing costs has been in your possession, i.e., in a bank account or investment account for a period of time. The minimum is almost always six months, with occasional exceptions to three months.

Stacking the File or The Stacking Order: You probably won't hear this one, but I'll include it just the same. Every Lender has its own stacking order, which is the order in which all your documentation is placed when the file is submitted. This is the last thing the Processor will do before "shipping" the file to the Lender and Underwriter.

TIL: ("Till") – Truth-in-Lending Disclosure. Originators love this one almost as much as "GFE." You will probably hear, "Well, I'm going to run a "till" for you and you'll be able to see exactly what we're charging you for your mortgage." Heads-up!! The

TIL you receive when you apply is not the final TIL (from the closing) and won't tell you anything really. And, the TIL doesn't tell you about what you are being charged by the mortgage company. That's the HUD. The TIL explains the amount of interest and calculates the annual percentage rate and finance charges. At this stage, like the GFE, it's an estimate only.

VOD, VOE, VOM, VOR – Verifications: The "VO" stands for Verification of. The D is Deposit. E is Employment. M is Mortgage. R is Rent. The Processor is required to send out the Verifications in writing to your bank, employer, mortgage company, or landlord. This creates a **slow-down point** which you can help shorten by being prepared. This is covered in greater detail in the chapter on Verifications.

YSP, Yield Spread Premium, Back-End Commission: Never in a million years are you going to hear either "YSP" or "Yield Spread Premium" unless you bring it up. Although it is no longer a mortgage lending term, it's still there. Now it's called (on the documentation) "Credit or charge (points) for the specific interest rate chosen." No matter what it's called, it is the commission the mortgage company earns by selling you a higher rate. This term is one of the most valuable in your jargon arsenal. Most mortgage companies will tell you that this is (a) not used any longer (because the name has been changed), or (b) confidential. It's not confidential at all. It is disclosed on the HUD-1 – in Section 800 and, even better, on the Comparison Page.

CHAPTER 6: THE APPLICATION

The objective of this chapter is to help you properly complete the Uniform Mortgage Loan Application – the Ten-Oh-Three. The form is challenging because it is, in many places, ambiguous. Hopefully, my explanations will clear that up for you.

FNMA (Fannie Mae) Form 1003 – FHLMC (Freddie Mac) Form 65: Here is the very first challenge, assuming you didn't find the jargon challenging. Google "FNMA 1003" and look for the www.efanniemae.com links. There are two versions: a printable, complete-by-hand version, and an electronic fill-able PDF version.

A fill-able, savable, printable form is included with the reader's document package.

Once you have your form, read along and fill in as you go.

Let's get started.

At the top of Page One, you will see a paragraph of language and two check boxes. Now then - whether to check or not check the two check boxes in this first section. Let me deal with the second box first. If you and another person are applying for the mortgage loan together and both of you intend to live in the house, using both of your assets, then the second box (right before the words "the income or assets") should be checked. In this instance, you would also check the first box. So for two Borrowers who will be owning the home together, both boxes are checked. If, on the other hand, there is a co-Borrower (common language is co-signer) who will not be living in the house nor be a co-owner of the property, only the first box is checked. There are times when only the first box is checked, or both boxes are checked. There would never be a time when only the second box is checked.

I. Type of Mortgage and Terms of Loan

In most cases, you will be checking the box marked "Conventional." If you are a Veteran and wish to apply for a VA (Veterans Administration) guaranteed loan, check VA. If you want to apply for an FHA (Federal Housing Authority) guaranteed loan, check that box.   USDA/Rural Housing Service applies to certain areas of the country (not always rural by the way) – ask your real estate agent or company if there are USDA programs available. FHA, VA, and USDA are not Investors. Rather, they are more like mortgage insurance companies: they guarantee repayment of the loan for its entire life. The "Other" will be for any loan that does not qualify as Conventional or one of the others. An example would be a non-conforming loan where the loan amount exceeds usual limits.   Google the term "Fannie Mae Conventional Loan Limits." This calls for a bit of explanation.   One- to four-unit homes (single-family, duplex, triplex, quad-plex) can all be financed conventionally. That web page shows you the limits for each as well as exceptions depending on geography.

Leave the Agency Case Number and the Lender Case Number blank. For now, we are going to assume that the home you are looking at will appraise for the sales price. In the current market, it should. Take the sales price of the home and deduct the amount of your down payment to arrive at the (Loan) Amount. Interest rate leave blank. Number of Months will be as follows: 30 Year Loan is 360, 25 Year Loan is 300, 20 Year Loan is 240, 15 Year Loan is 180, 10 Year Loan is 120. Enter the number of months – in most cases, 360.

In terms of Amortization, "Fixed Rate" is probably your best choice.

II. Property Information and Purpose of Loan

If you have a contract on a home, enter the complete property address. If not, enter "For Pre-Application Purposes Only." If you requested the Application from my site, you will be able to save your work. Number of Units is typically 1. However, it can be 2, 3, or 4 for duplexes and above. Ask your real estate agent for the Legal Description (also called a Metes and Bounds Description). You will enter this on the Continuation Page and note here, "See Continuation Page." Your real estate agent will know the year the home was built and this should be listed on the sales contract.

If you are applying for a refinance loan, enter your current address and put in the "legal description" – which will be detailed in your previous loan documents. And, you'll need to get out your previous HUD-1 Settlement Statement.

The Purpose of the Loan will either be Purchase or Refinance, usually. A Construction Loan covers the cost of construction without a final mortgage. If the loan program you are considering includes both the cost of the construction and the mortgage upon completion, then it's "Construction-Permanent." Other is just that – something beyond these four. Construction or Construction-Permanent may also cover rehabilitation or home improvement loans.

"Property will be:" If the home is where you will live the majority of the time, it is a primary residence. If a second home or vacation home, "Secondary Residence." If it is an Investment or Rental Property, "Investment."

The next line of boxes relates to Construction and Construction-Permanent Loans. Going from left to right: 1) What year did you buy the lot? 2) What was the sales price? 3) How much do you currently owe on the lot? 4) What is the Present Value of the lot (usually the same as the sales price)? 5) What are the projected construction costs (Improvements)?

The Total is the current value of the lot plus the construction costs.

The next line is for Refinance Loans (Refi's). 1) What year did you purchase the property? 2) What was the original sales price? 3) How much do you currently owe on the property (include all mortgages – first, second, home-equity, etc.)? 4) Purpose of Refinance – enter "R&T" (Rate and Term) or "C/O" (Cash-Out). 5) If you are going to do some improving to the property, list those (generally speaking) here, whether they have already been made or are to be made, and the cost or projected cost. Remember, even if you are only taking cash out of the property to cover the closing costs, it is still a C/O (Cash-Out) Refi.

"Title Will Be Held In What Names" – this is many times the Borrowers, but sometimes not. If two people are paying for the house together and living in the house together, both will be on the title and both names should be entered here. If there is a co-Borrower (i.e., a parent who is helping you buy your first home), you are on the title but not the parent, usually. The parent can be on the title – this is up to you. The Manner In Which Title Will Be Held varies from state to state – leave blank for now.

"Estate will be held in" is usually "Fee Simple," but not always. Leave unchecked for now.

Source of Down Payment, Settlement Charges and/or Subordinate Financing. This is a very important section in the application on purchases. Settlement Charges are Closing Costs. Subordinate Financing can be either the second loan in a combination program, or a loan from a family member to help with the down payment. If a purchase and the funds for the down payment and closing costs are in a savings account or other type of account, list the type of account, i.e., "Savings Account," "IRA," "Investment Account," etc. If a combination loan, list "Combination Loan." If help from a Family Member, list "Family Member" (this will have to be explained on the Continuation Page). If you are refinancing and will use part of the Loan Proceeds to cover the closing (settlement) costs, enter "Loan Proceeds." Do not leave this section blank.

Finally, it becomes a little easier.

III. Borrower Information

Generally speaking, put the higher income earner as the "Borrower," provided the income is documented. If the primary income earner is self-employed and much of the income is written off for tax purposes but the other Borrower has W2 income that is easily documented, you might put that person first. It's not supposed to matter but, many times, it does. Of course, if there is only one Borrower, the Co-Borrower section will be left blank. My preferred way of entering this information because it makes it easier for the Underwriter is like this: SMITH, Robert Charles. Last name in capitals, followed by first and then middle. The Fannie Mae form does not automatically insert dashes in the Social Security Number or the Phone so put those in. Nor does it enter the slash marks (/) for date of birth. Years of school is total years. High school graduate is 12. Bachelors degree is 16. And so on. It's important to answer the "Married" question accurately. If you are separated and in the process of getting a divorce, you need to check "Separated." A good Originator will review what that means exactly and what options you may or may not have depending on your state laws. The other two possibilities are obvious.

A dependent only needs to be listed once. This is a dependent living at home. If you have two children living at home and one child in college, although the child in college is in reality a dependent, you would only enter "2" and their ages. You won't list this again under Co-Borrower or you will end up with four dependents. So how do these differ? If the Borrower has a child from a previous marriage living with you, and the Co-Borrower has a child living with you, you would enter "1" under each of you with the corresponding ages.

Present Address is where you are living at the time of the application. Check Own if you are buying the home and Rent if you are renting. What if you are temporarily living with other family members rent free? Check Rent. We'll get to the costs later. As to number of years, calculate that to the best of your ability. If over two years and three months, put "3" and so on. If under two years, this needs to be entered as a decimal, i.e., 0.5 (six months), 1.3 (15 or 16 months), 1.9 (22 or 23 months). Mailing Address is left blank unless you have a different mailing address than your residential address, i.e., you live in a rural area and use a post office box.

There must be a two year residential history and I recommend three years. If you have been residing at your present address for less than two years, complete the next information block. Additional addresses with dates can be entered on the Continuation Page.

The Borrower and Co-Borrower information may be the same or it may be different. Enter the correct information for both people. This will show up on your credit report.

IV. Employment Information

This section begins on Page 1 and continues on to Page 2. I'll get to explaining that "If employed in current position for less than two years or ...." Put the complete mailing address for the employer here. If you are self-employed, enter the name and mailing address of your company and check the Self Employed box. This can become difficult when you own your own business and it is a large company (a corporation with many employees). Here's the rule of thumb: If you own 51% of the company or more, you are self-employed. If less, you are employed by the company. There are exceptions to this rule and finding a good Loan Originator who understands these will be more critical than usual. For "Years On the Job," if more than 2.5 years, enter 3. If in the third year, enter 4 and so on. If 14 months, enter 1.1 or 1.2. If two years and two months, enter 2.1 or 2.2.

Apply this same rule when answering "Years employed in this line of work/profession." When the time on job is less than two years, this is the first place the Underwriter will look – to see if the Borrower has changed jobs, staying in the same profession or industry.

Position/Title/Type of Business. If you are self-employed using the definition above, enter the "type of business." If you have a formal title, "Vice President of Marketing," put that. If you are a Records Clerk (Position), enter that.

Business phone is business phone – whatever telephone number goes to the "business."

Now on to the "If employed in current position ...."

If you have been on your job or owned your business for less than two years, enter information in this section. The dates "To" "From" can be entered month/year to month/year, i.e., 9/2010-6/2012. It's important to enter the four-digit year to make it clear for the Underwriter. Underwriters can whip through a well organized file in no time at all. The fewer potential questions the better. If, after completing the second employer box, you have more than two years, you can stop. If not, complete the next set as well. If you need to enter additional employers to get to two years, use the Continuation Page.

What if you work a part time job on the side or as a hobby. On my bio, I list that I build websites as an avocation. The revenue goes to my company, The Mazor Company, as does any revenue derived from my business. However, as a hobby, I deal fun casino games for parties. I work for this company and earn anywhere from $1500 to $2000 every year and have been doing so for the last five years. Would I enter that? Of course I would. To calculate the average monthly income, I would take my most recent 1099 and divide that number by 12. Does that get counted as income for purposes of calculating the debt-to-income ratios? Absolutely it does. I can prove up the income with my tax return.

And with that, we now get into Income, Assets, and Housing Expense. It is very important to get these numbers right. Many Originators don't, and then it bites everyone later when the Underwriter sends out a Conditions Notice wanting more information. Let's begin with Income.

V. Monthly Income and Combined Housing Expense Information

With this section, the idea of listing the easily verified or higher income earner as the Borrower might make more sense. First, please note that there are seven different income categories. It's important to get the right information in each of those and to make the entries as accurate as possible. Most people will only enter something in the first category, the "Base Empl. Income." If you are on a regular salary or hourly wage with predictable working hours, then enter your gross income here. Gross is before anything has been deducted (withholding, FICA, benefits premiums, retirement). This will be verified with paycheck stubs. What about people who work different hours each week or month? Go over your last 12 months of paycheck stubs and average your gross monthly income from those. Being exact in your entry (as opposed to estimating) gains points with the Underwriter. If you are self-employed, take your last six paycheck stubs, assuming you pay yourself a salary of some kind, and get an average of your gross earnings for those six months. It's going to be very important that those numbers be consistent with your most recent tax return and paycheck stubs/payroll history.

Now to the rest of the lines. Let's say you are a salaried employee but work overtime on a regular basis. "Regular" can be 5 hours per month to 50 hours per month. And you have at least a 12 month history of this. It's a pain but take out your paycheck stubs for the last 12 months or ask for a 12 month history from your payroll department. Hang on to these as you will need them later. Add up your overtime wages and divide by 12 to arrive at your monthly average. Enter that number in the line by Overtime.

Bonuses. Let's say you earn a regular salary but receive bonuses on a monthly, quarterly, semi-annual, or annual basis. Go over the previous 12 months and add up all of your bonuses, divide by 12, enter that number.

Commissions. If you are a commissioned salesperson and you are on a salary base versus a draw, then you will go over your last 12 months of commission, add them up, and divide by 12. If, on the other hand, you are on a draw, you will put everything under the Base line – again, 12 months of payroll history, total it, divide by 12 to arrive at an accurate monthly amount.

Do Underwriters ever require 24 months? Sometimes, especially when there has been a job change in the last two years. However, for entry purposes, use 12 months.

Dividends/Interest: If you have investment accounts and receive regular dividend payments, go back over the past 12 months, add up all your dividend earnings and divide by 12. Keep the statements handy.

Net Rental Income: Okay, this one is a bear. If you have rental property, to calculate your monthly income from that property, using the last 12 months (and you will need to supply some kind of breakdown preferably from your CPA), add up your receipts then subtract mortgage payments, taxes, insurance, maintenance, and other expense. Take the difference and divide by 12. But what if you are losing money? As painful as it is, you'll need to enter a negative dollar figure there. No, you can't just leave it blank. Your credit report is going to show your ownership interest in those properties. Leaving that blank is a red flag to the Underwriter. Assuming you are profitable, this is another income line. Later on, there will be an area of detailed entries and you will probably use those calculations to enter a number here.

Other: Here is where I would enter my fun casino earnings and the explanation would be entered in the next set of boxes. Now, total all those numbers up.

Go through this again for the Co-Borrower.

Do you have to provide a 12 month history? If you are claiming anything beyond a salaried, predictable income – yes. Although an Underwriter will many times accept three or six months, a 12 month history makes it clear. Think of it this way – you are the Underwriter and you want to make sure that everything makes logical sense. Even more than that, the Underwriter is going to understand that you arrived at your entries in an accurate manner.

Before we move on to Housing Expense, let's focus on that table that is titled, "Describe Other Income." This is where you explain entries from the "Other" line. In my application, I would enter the letter "B" since I would be the Borrower and then enter "Games Plus – part time fun casino company" and then enter the amount of my most recent 1099 from Games Plus and divide that by 12 to arrive at the monthly earnings. In terms of those who receive child support, spousal maintenance, or other things, you do not have to enter the information. However, it does improve your income and will improve your debt-to-income ratios. At the same time, you will have to document this either with a divorce decree, copies of recent checks from the person paying the support, or something similar.

Now – the Housing Expense entries:

If you are renting, put the amount of your monthly rent payment in that box. If you are not renting, leave it blank. If you are living with family rent free, enter "0" and an explanation on the Continuation Page.

If the home you are living in has a mortgage or mortgages, enter your principal and interest payment for each mortgage. Hazard Insurance is your monthly homeowner's insurance premium – enter that number. Real Estate Taxes are an annual figure. If you are not sure how much those are, you can visit your County Tax Assessor's website and find the annual amount – divide that by 12. If you are paying mortgage insurance, enter that number. If you live in a Homeowner's Association development, take your annual dues and divide that number by 12. Total it up.

Now to the right "Proposed" side. Much easier said than done. The reason is that, at this point in time, you don't know your interest rate and cannot accurately calculate the principal and interest payment on the new property. If you don't have a property yet, leave these blank for now. If you have a property in mind, and you know the price, and the amount of your down payment, then you can visit this website to calculate your monthly payment: www.mortgagecalculator.org. Note: that is ".org," not ".com." The good thing about this calculator is that it also gives you estimates (a bit on the high side) for mortgage insurance and property taxes. Rather than accepting the default amount for taxes, I recommend visiting your local County Tax Assessor's website, looking up the property you are interested in, and using the annual tax amount listed divided by 12. That will be completely accurate. If your down payment is less than 20%, include the mortgage insurance premium payment. By the way, the Tax Assessor's website will also have the "legal description" of the property.

Copy that and enter it onto the Continuation Page (Page 5) of the 1003.

Now, let's talk about the Hazard or Homeowners Insurance. The objective here is to be as accurate as possible. Call your insurance agent, provide him with the address of the property, and ask for a quote. Take the quote and divide by 12. If the property is in a Homeowners Association development, find out what the dues are, divide by 12, and enter that number.

The accuracy of these numbers is critical in determining the debt-to-income ratios. And the DTI ratios are critical to an Underwriter. Yes, you do get extra points for accuracy in most Underwriter's eyes.

VI. Assets and Liabilities

Although these are in the same section on the 1003, I'm going to go over each separately so we can focus on one at a time. Let's start with Assets.

By now, you know clearly whether this is a Joint (two Borrowers) or Not Joint (one Borrower) application. Check the correct box.

That "Cash deposit toward purchase held by" box tends to give Originators a great deal of grief because they don't understand it. What is being asked there is the amount of earnest money being held in trust and who is doing the holding. In all likelihood, if you are purchasing a home, you gave the real estate agent or company an earnest money check that was made out to the title company the real estate company works with most often. The "being held by" is the title company. The amount is the amount of the check. This will be credited toward your down payment and closing costs. If a refi, enter "N/A." If a purchase but you haven't found the right house yet, enter "Pending."

The next sections are for any savings, checking, or investment accounts that you have. Filling these out completely is very important – include the account number. One box for each account. Do not combine accounts. As to the balance, here you can approximate with the checking. However, be exact with savings and investments – as of the day you complete the 1003. Take out your last six months of statements for each account you list. If you have more than four accounts, include the others on the Continuation Page.

Continuing on to Page 3. There is one more box for bank accounts. Stocks & Bonds would be an investment account whether stocks, bonds, or a mutual fund. Again, use your most current value for the investment account and take out your last three quarterly statements. Under the "life insurance" section, what is being considered is a life insurance policy that has a "cash value" to it, i.e., whole life or universal life. Ask your insurance agent for a current statement. The "face value" is the amount that would pay in the event of your death. The current value is entered in the space where balances have been entered. Here's the beauty of using the Fannie Mae interactive form or in the readers document set. It is doing the math for you.

Real Estate Owned can be a little tricky. The next section gets into this so hold off on putting anything here for now. Vested interest in retirement fund is for an IRA, 401K or other retirement vehicle you have. You may have to contact your Human Resources department or investment advisor to obtain the value at the time of your application. You will need copies of the statements.

Net worth of businesses owned will be based solely on the value of the business according to its current financial statement. You may need a CPA to help you create this. Please note that any value entered will have to match the financial statement submitted with the loan application.

Automobiles – this one is fairly easy. List the current value of the vehicle (using the private party sales estimate from any of the blue book websites) LESS any liens against the vehicles. What if you are upside down? It happens. It is best – remember that this will show up on your credit report – to show the actual value. If the vehicle is worth $2,000 less than what you owe, show "-$2,000." If your vehicle is leased and there is a payout when the lease terminates, take that into consideration. Do not write in the word "leased." That is a red flag to an Underwriter.

Other assets include household furnishings – what is the replacement value? Art, jewelry, antiques, and other things of monetary value are entered separate from household furnishings.

And now you have your total assets. Let me cover the liabilities before I get into the entire real estate owned schedule. So let's go back to Page 2 on the right side of this section.

In this section, what not to include is as important as what to include. Do not include utility bills, cell phone bills, or other regular monthly bills that are not credit related. In the end, your Originator is going to import your open accounts to the "final" (which isn't really the final) 1003. It will be this one that gets submitted to underwriting. So, why are we going to all this trouble? Because this is going to help you take control of the mortgage process with the Originator or Broker. You have done your homework and that means that the mortgage company is going to have to deal with you in an up and up way. Also, with a good Originator, having done this indicates that you are committed to getting the best program you can.

To the Liabilities. Start with your credit cards. List the financial institution and the address to which you make payments, the account number, how much you usually pay on the balance each month, and the total outstanding balance.

Unlike the assets, you won't need copies of statements for this. Why? Because it is going to show up on your credit report. So, accuracy is important. For months left with credit cards, enter an "R" for revolving. Also, keep credit card charges and other revolving credit account use to a minimum until the mortgage process is completed. Why? Because it will cause your scores to drop. In other words, wait until after the closing to go buy furniture.

After you have entered the credit cards, enter any loans you have against vehicles you own. Calculate how many months you have left on these loans and enter that number. After that, enter any revolving accounts you might have with, as an example, a furniture finance company. If the finance contract is for a fixed number of months, enter the number of months left on the contract. If revolving, enter an "R".

Under income, spousal maintenance and child support receipts were optional. Not under liabilities. And yes they are calculated into the bottom or back-end DTI. Specify what the obligation is in the left hand box and the amount (monthly) in the right hand box. Job Related Expense is anything that is regular and predictable – good examples are provided such as "union dues" and "child daycare."

And now the 1003 is going to calculate your total assets, your income, your liabilities, and your net worth. We are going to manually calculate the debt-to-income ratios later on using the numbers generated over the last couple of pages.

Real Estate Owned

This is the most confusing part of the entire form and I have heard multiple explanations as to how to complete this section. I'll do my best to explain it for you.

First, enter the physical address of the property. You don't need the legal description – just the physical address. You are given three options as to how it is that you have this property. Notice that, "We have it on the market" isn't one of those options. If you have a home that you have sold and are using proceeds from that sale to purchase the house for which you are securing a mortgage at this time, enter the "S" (Sold). If you have a house that is under contract, enter the "PS" (Pending Sale). And if you have a house that is a rental property, enter "R" (Rental). If the house you are living in now is listed with a real estate agent or company, obtain a copy of your listing agreement for the file. If your house is on the market but not sold, you will be required to show that you can support the payments on both that house and your new home. If you are applying for a refinance loan and you have no other property, then there is nothing to enter here.

On to the type of property and calculations. The types of properties are: SFH (Single Family Home), 2-plex (duplex), 3-plex (triplex), 4-plex (quad-plex), Land, and Lot. If you own commercial property, that will probably relate to your business and will show up on the financial statement you will be including. If it is not within a business structure, then list it as whatever it is.

List the present market value as accurately as you can estimate it. Review your last three statements (yes, you will be including those for submission to underwriting) to determine the amount of principal still owing on the property. If you are receiving rental income, go over the last 12 months and add up the total earnings over that time period and divide by 12. This is the best way to arrive at an accurate estimate of what the future rental earnings will be. The mortgage payments will show up on the 12 monthly statements. Now, it starts getting tricky. For insurance, maintenance, taxes, and miscellaneous, we are going to also use the 12 month average. So create a table or spreadsheet with the last 12 months of rental receipts, mortgage payments, insurance payments, property taxes, maintenance expense, and other things (miscellaneous). Total it all up and divide by 12. Keep the table or spreadsheet handy – the Underwriter is going to want to see it. HINT: Rather than listing "Property Taxes," list the County. List the Insurance Company. List the maintenance companies. In other words, provide as much detail as you possibly can. The following lists the information an Underwriter will want:

PROPERTY ADDRESS:	1171 Siebert Lane
	Aurora, CO
CURRENT VALUE:	$128,550.00
MONTHLY PI PAYMENT:	$377.33
MONTHLY TAXES:	$82.21
COUNTY	Denver
HAZARD INSURANCE:	$71.81
INSURANCE AGENCY:	Allied Insurance
	2212 Porter Avenue
	Denver, Colorado
	303-555-5555
AVERAGE MAINTENANCE:	$14.81
MAINTENANCE COMPANY:	United Construction
	7712 Singleton Road
	Aurora, Colorado
	303-555-5555
RENTAL INCOME:	$675.00
MONTHLY EXPENSE:	$546.16
NET INCOME:	$128.84

Now, also notice that there is no fill-in area for Gross Rental Income. There is one for "Net Rental Income" but not for Gross Income. So, using that spreadsheet you just created, enter the bottom line Net Rental Income. And now, scroll back up to Section V. Monthly Income and enter your total Net Rental Income in that square.

The "Alternate Name" section doesn't mean what it says. If you have recently changed your name, and you have credit with a company that had the previous name (or still does), then indicate which account you are referencing. This becomes a challenge for newly married couples. If there are more than two, note the others on the Continuation Page. The more complete this is, the easier the underwriting.

VII. Details of Transaction and VIII. Declarations – HMDA (Hum-dah)

First, the transaction details. Purchase price is for a purchase. Alterations, improvements, repairs are for refinance, construction or construction-permanent loans. Refinance is for a refinance loan. The "(incl. debts to be paid off)" is for cash-out purposes. A few years back, it was common for Borrowers to refinance their home and pay off their credit card debt. Since there is little equity in most homes these days, this is not so common. If you are taking cash out of your home to pay off your credit cards, vehicle loans, or other things, I'm going to ask you to think about this for a second. You are paying off an obligation that can be eliminated in two or three years and moving that obligation into, in most cases, a 30 year loan with all the interest involved. Consider the difference in the out-of-pocket expense over time.

The Estimated prepaid items (also called "reserves") are going to be insurance premiums and property taxes (the calculations are based on the time of year you are buying and how much needs to be put into the escrow fund at closing. Estimated closing costs can't be calculated properly until you have seen the Good Faith Estimate. PMI, MIP, Funding Fee is best calculated by the Originator. Discount leave blank. Total costs – add it all up. In summary on this part, put in the Purchase Price, Construction Costs, or Refinance Amount and stop there.

And now the Declarations and the five questions I always hated to ask but had to. The answers to these questions will all appear on your credit report. Let me translate the questions into plain English:

a. Are there any outstanding judgments against you? Have you been sued, lost, and the company or person you owe filed a judgment against you? This includes tax liens, student loan liens, and judgments. Note that a condition to closing will be, assuming you get an approval, satisfying the judgment because an outstanding judgment will result in a lien against the property.

b. Have you been declared bankrupt within the past 7 years? Did you file bankruptcy and was it discharged in the past 7 years? Note that bankruptcies stay on the credit report for at least 10 years.

c. Have you had a property foreclosed upon or given title or deed in lieu thereof in the last 7 years? The foreclosure part is obvious. There is an alternative to foreclosure – to voluntarily give the deed to the Lender who holds the mortgage before you can be foreclosed on. Same deal – same effect.

d. Are you a party to a lawsuit? This includes a divorce. It's a lawsuit. This includes if you are suing someone or being sued over a car accident. Any lawsuit.

e. Have you ever directly or indirectly been obligated on any loan which resulted in foreclosure, transfer of title in lieu of foreclosure, or judgment? Have you ever had a loan, or co-signed for a loan of any kind, that ended up in default where a judgment, repossession, or foreclosure resulted?

I am going to cover Letters of Explanation in detail in the next chapter. Anywhere that you checked "yes" will require a Letter of Explanation.

To the Top of Page 4 - left side first. These things you won't be able to complete until you are working with the Originator. Back to the right side:

a. Are you presently delinquent or in default on any Federal debt or any other loan, mortgage, financial obligation, bond, or loan guarantee? Delinquent means late. Default means really late. The question is very broad and encompasses just about any kind of financial obligation – note the word "Federal" (student loans and federal income taxes).

b. Are you obligated to pay alimony, child support, or separate maintenance? Easy enough – if the answer is "yes," that means you'll need to supply a copy of the divorce decree that shows that and also include a Letter of Explanation. An alternative to providing the decree are copies of the most recent six months of payment checks.

c. Is any part of the down payment borrowed? Anytime a Borrower takes out any kind of loan to cover the down payment or closing costs, the answer to this is "yes." It can be an unsecured personal loan. It can be a loan against an investment account or life insurance policy. It can be a loan from a family member. This has to be disclosed. How will the Underwriter know? It will show up on the credit report. Or, there will not be enough money in the existing bank accounts to cover the down payment and closing costs. A loan against an investment account or life insurance policy may be approved. The personal loan will not be. The family member loan, many times, will be acceptable depending on the terms of repayment. If the loan is "forgivable" meaning it never has to be repaid, that is almost always acceptable. If the loan is only due upon sale of the property, that is usually acceptable. If, on the other hand, it is a loan requiring repayment on a monthly or even yearly basis, the Underwriter is going to want to know all the details.

d. Are you a co-maker or endorser on a note? This is asking if you have co-signed for anyone. If the answer is yes, that obligation will have to be noted with a Letter of Explanation and it may, depending on the payment history, be taken into account with your DTI ratios.

e. Are you a U.S. citizen?

f. Are you a permanent resident alien? This is asking specifically if one of the Borrowers is a Legal Permanent Resident.

g. Do you intend to occupy the property as your primary residence? Followed by, "If yes, complete question m below."

h. Have you had an ownership interest in a property in the last three years? If yes, then complete the next two lines.

Does this matter? Yes. An Underwriter is looking at two things: 1) Are you buying a home to live in or as an investment? and 2) Is there a mortgage history to verify?

IX. Acknowledgement and Agreement

This is what I call the "fine print." I want to specifically call your attention to the following language: "fine or imprisonment or both under the provisions of Title 18, United States Code, Sec. 1001, et seq.; (2) the loan requested pursuant to this application (the "Loan") will be secured by a mortgage or deed of trust on the property described in this application"

A few years ago, mortgage fraud resulted in a slap on the wrist. Since the foreclosure crisis, enforcement with regard to mortgage fraud has escalated. What Underwriters are especially sensitive to is the idea of attempting to finance an investment property as a primary residence.

X. Information for Government Monitoring Purposes

There are two sections here. The first is looking at demographics in terms of race and gender. You have the option of not furnishing the information. However, and now to the second section, if you elect not to furnish the information and this is done in front of an Originator, he is required to complete it. That is not the reason for the four check boxes under the "To be Completed by Loan Originator:" The loan Originator is verifying that all of the questions in the HMDA section were asked and answered out loud.

We are almost finished with the 1003, one more section to go – something I have referred to many times and once I cover the important points there, we get to move on.

<u>Continuation Page/Residential Loan Application</u>

First, add any information that was omitted earlier in the application. For example, you might put the legal description of the property first. Then, if a parent or other family member is helping out with the down payment, list the person, the relationship, and the nature of the arrangement, i.e., gift, loan, loan to be paid back upon sale of the property, or forgivable loan. Let me explain these terms a bit. When a family member helps out with the down payment, that help can come in four ways. A gift is a gift. The family member is "gifting" or "giving" you the money for the down payment. A loan is just that and you will need to explain the repayment terms. If you are paying $100.00 per month toward that, that will be calculated into both of the DTI ratios because it is a housing related expense. A loan to be repaid upon the sale of the property is, usually, a no-interest loan that is repaid if and when you sell the house. If there is interest, you will need to explain the interest agreement, i.e., simple interest of 6.00% annually. Here's an example. Your family member is loaning you $10,000 toward the purchase of a home and is charging you 6.00% simple interest. $10,000 X 6.00% = $600 per year. Interest is being added to your obligation on a basis of $50.00 per month or $600.00 per year. This is reasonable and an Underwriter won't have a problem with it usually. It needs to be explained, however; otherwise you will end up with a Condition. Finally, a "forgivable loan" is just that. It is a loan that may have interest attached to it but your family member is agreeing to "forgive the loan" making it a gift.

Where does this become an issue? It is critical with an FHA application. There are specific guidelines regarding down payment assistance from a family member.

It also helps to reference the area of the 1003 for which additional information is being provided. For example, using a loan from a family member, you might enter, "VIII.h. I am borrowing $2,500 from my parents to help with the down payment. This is a forgivable loan." One more note – ask your family member for six months of bank statements (seasoning) for the account where the loan money is held.

If you run out of room on the 1003 Form, continue with a text document. Later, I am going to recommend putting the 1003 on a flash drive. The text documentation continuation should be included also.

NOTE: NEVER TRANSMIT A COMPLETED 1003 BY EMAIL.

CHAPTER 7: VOs, LOEs, and SEASONING

Verifications were mentioned in the chapter on Jargon and the last chapter. The information for those should be included on the Continuation Page (Page 5) of the 1003. Why? Because this speeds up the process. In the very beginning, I identified a number of **slow-down points**. This is the biggest one.

The abbreviations for Verifications are: VOE, VOD, VOM, and VOR. The VO is "Verification of." The last letter tells you the what – Employment, Deposit, Mortgage, Rent.

Verification of Mortgage: (if you currently have or have had a mortgage in the last three years)
Wells Fargo Bank
123 Main Street
Anywhere, USA 00000
555.555.5555
Account Number: 000-00-0000-0000

Or, it may be this one or that could be "and" this one:

Verification of Rent:
ABC Apartments
123 Main Street
Anywhere, USA 00000
555.555.5555

List every landlord you have had in the last three years.

Verification of Deposit:
Wells Fargo Bank
123 Main Street
Anywhere, USA 00000

555.555.5555
Account Number: 000-00-0000-0000

List every financial institution and checking or savings account you have. If you listed investment or retirement accounts on page 3 of the 1003, list those details here.

Verification of Employment:
[Name of Borrower]
ABC Company
123 Main Street
Anywhere, USA 00000
555.555.5555
Contact: Jennifer Smith (usually human resources, payroll, or a supervisor)

[Name of Co-Borrower]
ABC Company
123 Main Street
Anywhere, USA 00000
555.555.5555
Contact: Robert Wilson (usually human resources, payroll, or a supervisor)

If you are self-employed, add this one:
Certified Public Accountant:
John Smith, CPA
123 Main Street
Anywhere, USA 00000
555.555.5555
Contact: [Name of Accountant Who Handles Your Business/Personal Tax Matters]

So what is the purpose of these? Are these things the Originator needs? No, and most Originators forget to ask for this information. This is for the Processor who has to verify employment, mortgage history, rental history, and the deposits (amounts and how long the money has been in the accounts which is "seasoning"). The Processor will send out forms to each entity listed, requesting a verification of the accuracy of what has been entered on the 1003 as well as payment history for mortgage and rent. You have just made the Processor's job a breeze. It's like I said: most Originators don't bother asking, so you end up receiving a call from the Processor. How many days does it take to get the file from the Originator to the Processor? It can take up to two weeks. How long does it take to get the Processor to call? It depends on her workload. How long does it take to then send out the Verifications – a day, two at most. You have just saved yourself a ton of time and a lot of grief.

Letters of Explanation:
Now what if – and this happens – you answered one of those questions in the HMDA section with a "yes." Ignoring it is not an option. In that Approval With Conditions, if there was a yes, there will be a Condition of "Letter of Explanation for Question f in the HMDA." So (a) what is a Letter of Explanation and (b) how do you write one of those?

A Letter of Explanation is exactly as it sounds. You don't need to write a 17 page letter, or even a 2 page letter; a single page will work very well. The most common "yes" answer in the HMDA comes from Question b, "Have you been declared bankrupt within the past 7 years?" This is what the Letter of Explanation would look like:

> Your Street Address
> City, State, Zip Code
> Current Date

To Whom It May Concern:

In [Month], [Year], I (or we) were forced to declare bankruptcy. As it happens, [name] became ill with [disease] and the cost of medical treatment became so great that we were unable to afford it. The obligations became unmanageable and, as a result, our only option was to file for Chapter 7 (or 13) Bankruptcy.

Since then, we have managed our money very well as you will see from our credit history and have not over-extended ourselves. We believe we are financially able to sustain the ownership of a home at this time.

Sincerely
[BORROWERS' SIGNATURES]

This is the basic form of any Letter of Explanation. State the when, state the what, explain how the what happened. Then go on to say that the problems have since been corrected and home ownership and a mortgage are realistic at this time.

If you answered yes to the co-signature question, explain who you co-signed for, your relationship to that person, your reasons for doing so, and that the other person's payment history has been on time and consistent. I would recommend, by the way, obtaining a payment history on any co-signed accounts for the entire history of the obligation. This may have an effect on your DTI (Debt-to-Income) ratio. That will be at the Underwriter's discretion. However, an ounce of prevention – showing an on-time payment history may take that out of consideration. There has to be a history. If the account has only been open a month or two, that won't be adequate – you'll need at least six months and possibly a year for there to be no consideration.

In the Letter of Explanation, explain the reason that a co-signer was necessary, i.e., your son was buying his first vehicle and had no credit history. As such, you chose to help him by co-signing on the car loan.

Any "yes" answer with the exception of Questions "j" through "m" requires a Letter of Explanation.

<u>Seasoning:</u>

There was a major case in Wisconsin a few years back (Wisconsin? It will make sense in a minute) where a company through its employees was buying up a great deal of real estate – mostly fixer-upper kinds of homes. The homebuyer had the money. The mortgage companies pushed through the loans. Everybody seemed happy. Except for the Drug Enforcement Administration who would have been alerted to a problem much earlier if the Originators, Processors, and Underwriters had done their job and verified "seasoning." The real estate buying company from Wisconsin was a front for a drug organization and they were using the properties to launder money. So, what is seasoning? It is how long the money for the down payment and closing costs has been in the accounts specified by the Borrowers. The usual requirement is six months, sometimes three.

Here comes a question. But what if the money for the down payment is coming from an inheritance? And many times it does. What do you do? You produce a copy of the Will and any probate documentation you have. You aren't going to like this one but I also recommend producing a copy of the Death Certificate. If you are not the executor, ask the person who is for a copy of both – she or he will have both and should provide those if you ask nicely. If you get a, "What do you need those for?" say the mortgage company requested them. It's not an unreasonable request if the money hasn't been seasoned for at least three to six months.

What if the down payment is a gift or loan from a relative? Then, you will have to provide the documentation that verifies the seasoning and a Letter of Explanation explaining that the relative (with the nature of the relationship) is gifting or loaning you the down payment. Tell your relative that she or he is going to have to produce six months of bank statements showing where the money was being held or how it came into her possession.

In the chapter after next, I'm going to go into support documentation. In this case, even though it will be verified, for any account with down payment and closing costs money, get six months of bank statements. This is also true for investment account statements – which are usually quarterly. Get the last two quarterly statements; three if it takes three to provide a six month history. The better and more thoroughly you are prepared, the faster the process will run.

As an aside, in a typical mortgage loan process, the Originator will ask for some of what is needed but not all. So the Originator or Processor calls you and asks for more information or documentation. That takes time. Getting the information to the Processor takes time. You are going to have it all – and then some. And that's how a file moves quickly. Step behind the eyes of a Processor for just a moment. Assume she has 20 files on her desk (which is not unusual for a good Processor). Which file gets her attention first? Yours, because the other files will require phone calls and follow-up. Your file is ready except for a couple of steps - requesting verifications, stacking, and submitting.

CHAPTER 8: THE CREDIT REPORT and CALCULATING RATIOS

Credit Reports

You will need to obtain a copy of your tri-merge credit report. There are three (the "tri" in tri-merge) credit reporting agencies called repositories. They are Experian, Equifax, and TransUnion. You can purchase a single report from any of them. However, that is neither the "tri" nor the "merge." "Merge" means that all three reports are "merged" into one report. The tri-merge is all three agencies in one.

Back when I was still an Originator, Equidata was a popular resource for mortgage companies. At that time, their services were not available to the public. I don't know how they are today because I haven't worked with them. You may find the link www.equidatacreditservices.com helpful. There is an option to purchase a Three Bureau Report which should be the tri-merge. I also recommend doing some searching on your own. Obtaining your complete (tri-merge) credit report is an important step in this process.

The tri-merge report has three scores, displayed on the first or second page of the report. The Lender will pay attention to the middle of the three scores, commonly called the "mid-score." Your scores will be an important piece of information on your Mortgage Loan Summary.

Debt-to-Income Ratios (DTI)

There are two debt-to-income ratios. The top or front-end, and the bottom or back-end. The top ratio is housing expense versus income. The bottom ratio is all credit obligations including the proposed housing expense versus income. A loan Originator is not interested in the financial numbers (income and expense), only in the percentages. So let us calculate. All the numbers you need are in the 1003. You even have an estimated new housing payment. If you did your homework, you have a pretty good idea of what your taxes are going to be and what the homeowner's insurance payment will be. If you used the website I recommended, you even have an estimate of the mortgage insurance if needed.

The Top Ratio: Take the amount of your total projected housing expense and divide that into your total gross income. As an example, your projected total housing expense is $527.81 and your total gross income is $3,750.00. The formula looks like this (I know it sounds backwards): 527.81 ÷ 3750 which equals 0.1407 which is 14.1% (the fourth digit – the 7 is greater than 4 so the 0 is rounded up to 1). That percentage is your Top DTI ratio.

The Bottom Ratio: Take the amount of your total monthly liabilities (listed on the 1003) plus your projected housing expense. Add them up, then divide that number into your gross income. Using the same example above: $527.81 (Housing) + $377.66 (Other Obligations) = $905.47. 905.47 ÷ 3750 = 0.2414 or 24.1%. That percentage is your Bottom DTI Ratio.

For what it's worth, the Originator is looking for a top of less than 25% and a bottom of less than 45% (sometimes 50%). However, there are exceptions to these rules.

Loan to Value Ratio (LTV)

The first number that you have to have is the appraised value of the home. If you haven't had an appraisal done yet, then go with the purchase price for now. The controlling number is the lower of the two. That is the number used in calculating the LTV. As an example, if you buy a house for $100,000 and you are putting $10,000 down, it would seem logical that your LTV would be 90%, and it is. However, if you are buying a home for $100,000 and it appraises for $98,000, then the LTV changes.

Let me explain the calculations as an Underwriter wants it explained. What is the loan amount? In this example, it is $90,000. What is the value of the home? Using the lesser appraisal figure from the previous paragraph, it is $98,000. The loan amount divided into the appraised value produces a percentage of 91.8%. That would be the LTV. The formula looks like this: $90,000 ÷ $98,000 = 0.9183 or 91.8%. Of course, if the home appraises for $100,000 or more, then the LTV is 90%.

But what if the home appraises for $105,000? Sorry – the lesser of the two. Although an improved appraisal will help later with mortgage insurance elimination, it doesn't help at the purchase stage.

Combined Loan to Value Ratio (CLTV)

Again, the most important number to consider will be the appraised value of the home. Lacking that, use the purchase price. A combination loan, sometimes called a "piggy-back," is literally two loans in one transaction. The purpose of this is to eliminate the mortgage insurance requirement.   Typical expressions for a combination loan program are: 80/10/10, 80/15/5, 80/20.   I doubt there are any 80/20 (no down payment, 100% financing programs) available but there used to be.

Let me break this down further for you. An 80/10/10 is an 80% first mortgage, a 10% second mortgage, and a 10% down payment. This assumes the house will appraise for the purchase price or higher.   An 80/15/5 is an 80% first mortgage, a 15% second mortgage, and a 5% down payment.

With combination loans, the measurement of the value of the obligation or the indebtedness is called a "combined loan to value ratio" or CLTV. With an 80/10/10, the CLTV is 90% - 80% + 10%. With an 80/15/5, the CLTV is 95% - 80% + 15%.

Again, this assumes the house will appraise at the purchase price of the home or higher. What happens if it doesn't? Let's take the $100,000 house that appraises for $98,000. You are considering, with an 80/10/10 program, an $80,000 first mortgage and a $10,000 second mortgage. The total financing then is $90,000. Divide that into the $98,000 appraised value and the CLTV becomes 91.83%. With most combination loans, the requirement is to stay accurate with the percentages. The CLTV cannot exceed 90%.

The Lender will change the parameters of your loan to $78,400 (80% of $98,000 – the appraised value) for the first mortgage and $9,800 (10% of $98,000) for the second mortgage. Your CLTV remains at 90%. However, you will have to have $9,800 for the 10% down payment and an additional $2,000 (the difference between the purchase price and the appraised value. So your down payment becomes $11,800 instead of $10,000 plus the closing costs.

A word of caution about combination loans. The second loan is almost always an adjustable rate loan, meaning that the interest rate could rise over time. Seldom are these fixed-rate loans. As well, even though mortgage insurance premiums are an additional expense, they will disappear over time with increased equity and a reduced loan-to-value ratio. The second loan in the combination is with you for 30 years as is the case with the primary loan.

CHAPTER 9: THE REQUIRED DOCUMENTATION

Now we come to all of the documentation that you will want to collect and organize before visiting with a mortgage company. As I was generating this list, I realized a couple of important things. First, this is a lot of paper. Obtaining it is a pain. Keeping it organized is a bigger pain. The easiest way to do this is to go to an office supply store and buy an expandable file wallet and file folders. I also recommend file folder labels so that you have everything well organized for yourself, the Originator, and (most important) the Processor.

The end result of all this organization is a happy Processor and potentially a confused Loan Originator as in, "Uh? How did you folks know that all this stuff was needed? Have you been to some other mortgage company already? I mean, I'm confused because nobody ever brings in all these things." By the way, that's true. No Borrower ever brings in everything in the beginning.

Most important, this level of preparation and organization strengthens your bargaining position. You have just saved the Originator and the Processor a great deal of time, and time is money.

Here's the list:

The Mortgage Loan Summary: This is one of the last items in the book but first in your stack of documentation. Why? Because this is what you are going to hand to the Loan Originator before anything else. You'll understand once we get there.

<u>Purchase Contract OR Most Recent HUD-1 Settlement Statement</u>: A copy of your Purchase Contract if you are buying a home. A copy of the HUD-1 if you are refinancing the mortgage on your home.

<u>The 1003</u>: This will be the copy you print out. The Originator is probably going to ask to see it. He may be wondering how complete and accurate it is. It will be both accurate and complete. Include the additional pages you created.

<u>Tri-Merge Credit Report</u>: After he has looked at the 1003, he'll want to see this.

<u>Bank Statements</u>: Statements from every bank account you have for the last six months. Generally speaking, the Processor will ask for two months. However, when it comes to support documentation, I'm a big believer in overkill. It's just easier in the long run. Staple each monthly statement together. Use a large paper clip to keep the statements for each account together. For most people that's two – checking and savings. But some people have more than two accounts. The staples keep the months organized. The paper clips keep the accounts organized. If you decide to go the file folders route, a separate folder for each account is best.

<u>Investment/Retirement Account Statements</u>: Statements from every investment account – including retirement accounts. Most investment accounts come in quarterly statements. Make sure you provide a six month history. If you have a retirement account with your employer, ask for copies of your last six months of statements if you don't get those automatically. Same deal – separate the months with staples and the accounts with a paper clip.

<u>Payroll Check Stubs</u>: Six months of payroll check stubs. Most people toss the payroll check stub right after separating the

check to take to the bank. Yes, I know that. Your payroll department can provide a six month payroll history.

Tax Returns: Two years if you are a W2 employee; three years if you are a 1099 contractor or you own your own business (with 51% of the ownership or more). If you own your own business, you will also need three years of your business tax returns

Letters of Explanation: If you have created one or more LOEs, include them.

Mortgage History Letter: If you currently have a mortgage, ask the Lender to provide you with a one-year payment history signed by an employee of the bank. This may eliminate the VOM.

Rental History Letter: If you are currently renting, ask your landlord for a one-year payment history letter. This may eliminate the VOR.

Employment History Letters: Ask your employer(s) for an employment letter, i.e., "John Smith has been employed with [name of company] for the past [term] in the capacity of [job position] (eliminating the VOE).

CPA Letter: If either Borrower is self-employed, ask your accountant or tax preparer for a letter explaining how you are self-employed, verifying your income, and verifying that this person has prepared your taxes and is familiar with your business.

Assets: You may own things that establish asset value. Are these necessary? No, but they come in handy. If the asset is real estate related, it was covered on the 1003. The objective is to identify the asset and its value. Examples include:

<u>Vehicle Registrations</u>:   Copies of the registrations for all vehicles

<u>Other Assets:</u> If you own antiques, there will be a rider to your homeowner's or renter's insurance policy, assuming you are insuring those above and beyond the usual policy. Include a copy of the rider because it shows the value. If you own art work, there will be a rider to your insurance policy. Include a copy of the rider. If you own jewelry, include a copy of the rider. If you own firearms, include a copy of the rider. If you own a boat, snowmobile, or other recreational vehicle, there will be separate policies for those. Include a copy of the Declarations Page from your insurance policy and copies of any registrations.

<u>Property Tax History</u>: Whether you are buying a new home or refinancing, visit the Tax Assessor's Office and request a copy of the property tax history. Although the tax payments came out of escrow, it's still a good idea to include this. If you own multiple properties, get one for each property you own.

<u>Homeowner's (or Renters) Insurance Policy:</u>   Include the whole thing. The purpose is to show that you have kept your home insured.

<u>Divorce Decree</u>: If you are receiving support, you'll need this to document the support. A second option is to provide copies of the last six support checks.

And that is a very nicely stacked file. Will you need all of this? Probably not. But all the documentation will come in handy just the same. The value comes from clearly demonstrating to the Originator that you are serious. That is absolutely golden. And it shows that you are not interested in playing games. You are there to obtain a mortgage on a home at the best possible rate with the most reasonable fees. After all, you are making the Originator's and Processor's jobs much easier. That should translate into savings.

<u>The Appraisal</u>: A word on Appraisals and we're in a bit of a Catch22 here. The Mortgage Company orders the appraisal, not the Borrower, not even with a Refi. If you have an appraiser you like, ask the Originator if his company will accept an appraisal from your appraiser. If the answer is yes, then go with your appraiser. If no, then ask who the mortgage company uses. The way to protect yourself here is to make sure that you tell the mortgage company that you will meet the appraiser when he inspects the home and that you will pay the appraiser. Why? Because if you pay the appraiser rather than the mortgage company, and then change mortgage companies, the appraiser is more likely to re-assign the appraisal to the new mortgage company. It also means that this fee has already been paid and doesn't need to be paid later at closing. The mortgage company may say, "Oh, there's no need for that. We'll pay for the appraisal and just include that in your closing costs." I don't recommend that because if you do change mortgage companies, you will have to pay for a second appraisal.

<u>The Survey</u>: If you are applying for a refinance mortgage, look in your closing package from when you purchased the home. There should be a certified copy of the Survey there. If you are purchasing, ask the Seller for a copy of the Survey. If these things fail, ask the real estate agent how to obtain a copy of the Survey. You may have to request a copy from the local Abstract Office.

CHAPTER 10: ASSEMBLING YOUR LOAN PACKAGE

The whole key to being "loaded for bear" as the saying goes, is organization. Mortgage Loan Processors are people just like the rest of us. They typically will work on the easiest files first and put off working on the files with challenges. In other words, the well-organized package requires little effort and moves faster than the file that requires phone calls, follow-up, and requests for additional documentation.

So the objective here is to do everything possible so that the Processor neither has to think nor work. All she will have to do is put it all together in the stacking order that the Lender wants and send it on.

In reality, the Processor will have to request Verifications. However, all of that information has already been provided on the 1003. She doesn't need to call and ask for the information which eliminates a major *slow-down point*. The letters from your mortgage company, landlord, and employer may save on two or three verifications.

If you have assembled everything using the overkill method, and six months of statements are needed, they are already there. She won't have to call you and ask you to provide additional statements.

If the end of a pay period occurs or another bank statement becomes available between when you have sent in your documentation and when it is processed and sent to the Lender, you already know it is going to be requested. You can send those to the Originator or call and ask how to get those to the Processor.

As I mentioned in the last chapter, in terms of assembly, I recommend purchasing a expandable file wallet (Google "Smead Expanding Wallet" to see an example) and file folders for each class of item and then placing everything in this order:

Mortgage Loan Summary

1003

Credit Report

Purchase Contract (purchase) or HUD-1 Settlement Statement (refinance)

Bank Statements (individual folder for each account)

Investment Account Statements (individual folder for each account)

Payroll Records (individual folder for each Borrower)

Personal Tax Returns (last two or three years)

Business Tax Returns (three years)

Homeowner's or Renter's Insurance Policy

Registrations for Vehicles Owned

Documentation for Other Assets Listed on 1003

Documentation for Other Property You Own (Property Tax Records)

Letters of Explanation

CPA Letter (if self-employed)

Appraisal

Survey

Although this may intimidate the Originator, it will make the Processor's job much easier. Easier processing means faster processing, which means faster closing.

CHAPTER 11: THE RIGHT MORTGAGE COMPANY

This is way easier said than done. I'll tell you where and how to start looking. Although I mentioned Linda Joyce in the Loan Officer chapter, I didn't include this story. L's office was literally across the hall from the title company that L used to close loans. N, the title officer, always kept her door open and L kept his door open. We could hear what went on over there and they could hear what went on in our office. I am guessing that N must have heard the discussion of, "But, we're lying." "No, just tell the customer it's a different program." As I was walking down the hall, N came after me. She said, "Pat – I really like you and your attitude toward business. Do you want to stay in the mortgage industry?" My response was, "Not if I have to do that." N said, "You don't have to. Here – call Linda Joyce. She is an honest and trustworthy mortgage broker. I think the two of you would get along very well." Linda and I did.

This is your best resource for finding a reputable mortgage company. If you have previously purchased a home, call the title company that handled the closing. Ask to speak to the title officer who worked with you. Be honest and upfront. Say that you are looking for a mortgage and that you thought she might be a good resource to ask about mortgage companies. If you know of someone who works for a title company, ask that person. If all else fails, Google "title companies" in your city, call, and ask to speak to a title officer.

A minor note of caution: some title companies prefer not to act as if they play favorites. In that case, most will say, "I'm really not permitted to do that. Sorry." It's worth a try.

The Mortgage Loan Summary

Now we come to a very important document. When I talked about the order of documents that you would have in your file, this was the first one – The Mortgage Loan Summary.

Let me explain where the idea came from. There is a thing known as a Loan Submission Form which a mortgage company will submit either electronically or by fax to a Lender. It gives an Underwriter a quick glimpse of the file from which an initial assessment and opinion can be given. The loan Originator knows what information is critical to an Underwriter and (hopefully) knows why.

Your Mortgage Loan Summary is going to offer the same "bird's eye view" to the Originator. This should be the first document you show an Originator once you have decided that you think you may have found the right company.

Everything should be self-explanatory. If you are requesting a Rate and Term (R&T) refinance with no cash out, circle "Refinance (R&T)." If you are requesting a Cash-Out (C/O), even if it is just to cover closing costs, circle that. Of course, with a refinance program, there is no down payment, although you will be obligated to pay the closing costs.

Mortgage Loan Summary

BORROWER:_____

CO-BORROWER:_____

CURRENT ADDRESS:_____

_____

SUBJECT PROPERTY:_____

_____

PURCHASE   REFINANCE(R&T)   REFINANCE(C/O)

PURCHASE PRICE/
CURRENT VALUE: _____

DOWN PAYMENT: _____

LOAN AMOUNT: _____

LTV and CLTV: _____

DTI: TOP   BOTTOM
                    _____   _____

                    Equifax   Experian   TransUnion

BORROWER SCORES_____

CO-BORROWER SCORES _____

SOURCE OF DOWN PAYMENT/CLOSING FUNDS:

_____

SEASONED FOR: _____ MONTHS

Key Questions To Ask Mortgage Companies

There are two sets of questions to ask. One is the set for when you are looking for a mortgage company. The second is the set for when you think you have found a mortgage company you can work with. Go into this with a mindset of you being an employer and asking yourself if you would hire this person to work for you. If the answer is "no," that should tell you something. If the answer is "maybe," then it could be maybe. If it is "yes," you may have found the right person. However, please keep in mind that at the heart of it all, you are dealing with a salesperson who works on commission and is motivated to make a positive first impression.

Questions to Ask While Searching

Begin by providing the Originator with enough information to get his interest. Here is what I recommend:

"Hello. My name is Pat Mazor and I am considering purchasing a home (or refinancing my home) and am looking for a mortgage company. Would you tell me about your upfront fees please? Specifically, I am asking about an application fee and your loan origination fee or mortgage broker fee."

You have been good enough to identify yourself by name and to state your reasons for calling. You have asked a question that is almost never asked but the answer is going to provide you with very valuable information. Keep in mind that those fees you just asked about go in the mortgage company's pocket.

Next question (assuming there is an application fee), "And is the application fee paid upfront and non-refundable?" If the answer to this question is yes, move on. This is a "hook."

If there is no application fee, the next question is, "How much do you charge for the credit report?" This is a throw-away question intended to put the Originator at ease.

Okay, one more question, "Will you allow us to pay the appraiser directly?" If the answer is "no," move on. This is a "hook." If yes, then, "What questions do you have for me?"

Where things go from here is unpredictable. In all likelihood, these questions have thrown the Originator for a loop. His initial reaction will be that he is being shopped by another mortgage company or a real estate agent or company, except that other loan Originators would never ask these questions. Answer what you feel comfortable answering. If you aren't comfortable answering a question, say so.

When you have finished the telephone conversation, rate the call using the following scale with 1 being least likely to want to hire and 4 being most likely to want to hire.

Fill-able PDF versions of this form and the Mortgage Company Query are included with the readers document package.

Mortgage Company Query

Name of Company:_____

Contact Information:_____

Name of Person Contacted:_____

Courtesy	1	2	3	4
Knowledge	1	2	3	4
Openness	1	2	3	4
Attitude	1	2	3	4
Professionalism	1	2	3	4

Pros:_____

_____

Cons:_____

_____

Comments:_____

_____

Recommendation: Create this form and print out at least ten copies so you can keep accurate notes about the companies you've contacted.

Make ten phone calls and then narrow down to three in-person visits. A mortgage is a huge investment – probably the largest and most important investment you will make. This is definitely the time to be doing a thorough job of shopping around. If you don't come away with three possible short-list companies, keep calling.

Questions to Ask When You Are Hoping You Have the Right Company

Make sure you bring all the documentation with you that was covered previously. Let me explain how mortgage companies take advantage of people and that will explain how you have an advantage. Imagine if you knew absolutely nothing about the mortgage process. You don't understand that the mortgage company has complete control over the majority of upfront fees with the exception of title fees, the credit report fee, and the appraisal fee. The processing fee may be something they have control over and may not. It depends on whether there is an employee who is a Processor. It's not worth arguing over either way. Any other fees (and you will see these on the Good Faith Estimate) are almost always fees that are generated by the Mortgage Company. That means they are negotiable.

When you decide to meet with a Loan Originator/Mortgage Company in person, set an appointment – a fixed time for meeting. This psychologically establishes structure, a good thing.

If you are an A-paper Borrower, that puts you in the strongest position. I'm guessing a mid-score above 720, top DTI below 25%, bottom DTI below 45%. LTV won't matter provided you aren't seeking something greater than 95%. If the mid-scores are lower than 720, or the DTIs higher than 25/45, it weakens your negotiating position. The position is strengthened by the fact that you can and will easily go elsewhere.

After the introductions and handshakes, hand the Originator the Mortgage Loan Summary. This does the following:

It provides the snapshot of the important points concerning your application and loan; it shows that you have done your homework and understand the process. Most important, it shows that you are taking the process very seriously.

The Originator may ask you about the documentation that you have with you. Be honest. Tell him that this is all the support documentation. That you have assembled it and, except for the appraisal, your loan should be ready to submit once a 1003 (Ten-Oh-Three) (use that term) has been input, and credit has been pulled and populated into the file.

A good Originator will see this as a huge plus. A poor Originator will be threatened by this level of preparedness. That should also tell you something.

Hopefully, you will have a good Originator who will ask something along the lines of, "So – how can I help you?"

Let's get the hardest part out of the way right now.

"Mr. Originator, we have worked very hard to prepare to apply for a mortgage on (or to refinance) our home. We have done a great deal of research. We believe that you should be fairly compensated. However, where we want to do things differently than most Borrowers is to have a say in 'how' you are compensated. We understand that most mortgage companies are compensated with fees that are disclosed on the GFE and then also with your back-end commission. We don't object to that at all provided the compensation is within reason. I mean, it doesn't really matter whether you are paid on the front or on the back just as long as you are paid adequately. Would you agree?"

This is a make or break question. If the Originator agrees, you are in luck. If you get a response like, "Well, how we are compensated is our business," then the best thing to do is move on because this company is not going to agree to transparency.

If the Originator agrees, then you can start putting something together. It's time to ask the money question. "Would you tell me approximately what percentage you would need to make on our mortgage?" Anything between 1.5% and 2.5% is reasonable. 2.5% to 3.0% - maybe. Over 3.0% - no. On jumbo loans (anything over $500,000), this goes down to 1.5% to 2.5%. On super jumbo loans (over $1,000,000) this goes down to 1.0% to 2.0%. Think about it – the amount of work that the mortgage company puts in is the same for a $150,000 mortgage or a $1,500,000 mortgage. If a mortgage company tells you differently, it's lying. The Originator is not going to be able to give you an exact figure unless you are prepared to pay the company's entire fee on the front end. Take your loan amount and multiply that by the top percentage you were given. And say, "So, you are expecting to make, at most, [that number] on our mortgage. Is that correct?"

Hopefully he says yes. Next question, "Are you willing to agree to that in writing?" Again, hopefully yes. If no, then you need to re-evaluate. I would recommend moving on.

The question now is whether you can afford to pay the entire fee upfront. If you can, you will be way ahead in terms of monthly payment and interest over the life of the loan. If you can't, it will be a matter of balance.

Then: "As I mentioned, we do not have a problem with you being fairly compensated and we agree that [whatever he said] is fair. We would like to pay as much of that upfront as we can so that we can keep the rate and P/I payment as low as possible. When it comes time to lock our rate, we will wait until we have a clear to close and hope you will tell us when you think we might save an eighth or quarter. Then, we'll come in and meet with you. We want to see the rate sheet that you will be using to lock our rate and to explain the back-end earnings or whatever you call your commission from the Lender, when we lock, so we can go over everything one more time making sure that we are in complete agreement. Would that be fair?" The Originator will probably not agree to show you the Rate Sheet. If he does, you just hit one out of the park.

If you are still in the same ballpark, then it's time to cinch the deal and get moving on the processing of the loan, "Here is our situation. When the HUD is ready 24 hours before the closing, we are going to go to the title company and review that to make sure that everything is as we have agreed throughout the process. If it is, we're fine and we'll close the next day. If it isn't, we will stop the closing. If all of this works for you, it works for us."

When dealing with an Originator, he may have to consult his manager or the owner of the company. These scenarios don't get presented very often. It is far from an everyday occurrence. The manager may just say "no dice."

The mortgage industry is not used to this level of transparency and accountability. You may have to do some pretty serious shopping to get this. However, it will save you a great deal of money – when done right, thousands of dollars.

There may be a situation where you get most of what you want but not all of what you want, i.e., a lack of willingness to show you the rate sheet. However, even if you don't get that, and you bring up the issue of reviewing the Settlement Statement before the closing, then you are probably in pretty good shape. When the Originator calls to ask if you want to lock your rate at whatever percentage, you can ask, "Fair enough – before I agree to that, tell me what your company's total revenue will be on our loan." If it's in the ballpark, then you have a choice. Frankly, I would follow that up with, "And when we review the HUD, this is what we'll see?" If you get a yes, you are in great shape.

So what happens if you review the Settlement Statement and it's not what was promised? First, the rate cannot be changed without your permission. If an Originator quoted you a rate and the rate changed, stop the closing and report the company to that state's governing agency for mortgage companies. If the HUD reflects earnings for the mortgage company that aren't in line with your agreement, you will have a choice to make. Be sure to point out your intentions to the real estate agent and to the seller during the process. There is a good chance that the real estate agent will call the mortgage company just to let them know you are serious. This is another way of keeping everything honest.

I want to warn you that this approach, and being armed with this information, is going to provoke defensive and aggressive behavior from less professional Originators and Brokers. Salespeople are taught to take control of the sales interview at the outset. Pointed, on target questions will threaten all but the best sales professionals – the top 10%.

Some examples of defensive/aggressive behavior might include sarcastic responses like, "Oh, so you already know all there is to know about mortgages it seems." Some Originators may tell you they aren't interested in working with you. Some may even hang up on you while you are attempting to get started. The thing to keep in mind is that you are weeding out the companies you don't want to work with.

I can say, with complete confidence, that Linda would have gladly disclosed all of the information outlined in this chapter to a client. Her philosophy, and mine as well, was that an educated borrower is a breeze to work with, will save a ton of time in processing and underwriting, and is worth a discount because of the time and effort savings.

CHAPTER 12: MORE TIPS and LOCKING YOUR RATE

In the previous chapter, I listed a number of questions to ask. In this chapter, I'm going to offer a different perspective – one based on how I would do things.

If I were applying for a mortgage today, and using the knowledge I have of the industry and the people in the industry, I would approach things with an eye toward making sure I use that knowledge to save time in the processing and, even more important, money on the front end and back end. In creating a list of ten possible mortgage companies, I would recognize that the majority are going to wash out on the first phone call. This is not a concern and is expected. The initial phone call will only take about a minute.

Stepping behind the eyes of the Originator salesperson for a moment, recognize that the majority of calls they get are from shoppers who are not going to want to disclose information. In counseling, there is a term known as "up-ending the expectations." The Originator's expectations are that nearly every phone call will be a shopper asking about rates – because that's what most people do. As was pointed out, the rate isn't locked in until the end of the process. So, why bother asking about rates? Rather, let's up-end the expectations with something like this. The Originator answers, "ABC Mortgage. May I help you?" and hears this in response, "Good morning. My name is Pat Mazor and I am shopping for a mortgage company that's willing to work with me and willing to be transparent as we move through the process. I am looking at a $223,000 mortgage with an 89% LTV assuming the appraisal proves up. My DTIs are 23% and 47%. My mid-score is 731. I have the down payment and closing cost money and can show it has been seasoned for seven months. I believe that gives you the information you need to know about whether I will qualify. I have not submitted an application to any company yet and would like to know if you can you tell me a little bit about how your company operates?"

In nine out of ten cases, this is going to throw an Originator so far off track that there will be a few moments of silence while he attempts to regain his bearings. You're not looking for the nine. You're looking for the one. As the phrase goes, you may have to kiss a few frogs before you get to the princess.

In thinking about this and about the possible responses, I kept coming up with one excellent response and how I would answer the question if I got a call like this. My response would be, "What is it that you would like to know?" A sales pitch tells us nothing. A statement like, "Wow, you've done your homework," tells us nothing. A question of, "Have you already applied somewhere else?" tells us very little. "What would you like to know?" indicates a willingness to work with the client. There are other positive responses as well. This is the one that I like because it opens the door to establishing a consulting relationship as opposed to a seller-buyer relationship. The key here is to be listening to the response with an ear toward trying to answer the question, "Is this someone I can work with and who will be dedicated to helping me?"

What do you want to know? Three things. First, what level of transparency is being offered? Second, how much does the company need to earn on your mortgage? Third, is the company willing to give you an opportunity to decide how that will be earned? In my opinion, these are all make-or-break issues. If the answer to any one of these is "No," then the best thing to do is move on to the next phone call.

Let me provide a model for how this conversation might go.

Client: Good morning. My name is Pat Mazor and I am shopping for a mortgage company that's willing to work with me and willing to be transparent as we move through the process. I am looking for a $223,000 mortgage with an 89% LTV assuming the appraisal proves up. My DTIs are 23% and 47%. My mid-score is 731. I have the down payment and closing cost money and can show it has been seasoned for seven months. I believe that gives you the information you need to know if I will qualify. I have not submitted an application to any company yet and would like to know if you can tell me a little bit about how your company operates?

Originator: What would you like to know?

Client: I recognize that you need to be compensated for the work you do. My real goal is to find a company that will allow me to have a say in how you are compensated – whether on front end fees or back end commission. Is that something you can do for me?

[This is definitely a make-or-break question. As well, at this point, you are going to have a pretty clear idea of whether this company is one that wants to help you or just wants your money.] You may hear something like this:

Originator: I don't get these kinds of phone calls very often. To answer your question, I think our company is one that will work with you the way you want. If I might, I'd like to ask how you know so much about mortgage loan origination.

Client: I read a book about the process and how to find a good mortgage company.

Originator: Okay. Yes, I would be happy to work with you and to be open about how we are compensated and to allow you to choose how to pay us.

Client: Can you tell me what range, in a percentage, you need to earn on my mortgage?

Originator: Somewhere in the 2% to 2.5% range usually.

This is another make-or-break point. If you hear something along the lines of, "That's confidential," or "We don't disclose that," it is a definite move on. If you want to have the last word, and nearly all of us do from time to time, you can say this:

Client: That's not at all true. It's going to show up on the HUD which I'm going to review as soon as it's available. Thanks very much for your time.

Going forward with our "in a perfect world" scenario:

Client: Okay, that sounds fair to me. Do you have any non-refundable upfront fees – other than the credit report?

If there is a non-refundable application fee, you can ask if he is willing to waive that in your case. As mentioned elsewhere, non-refundable upfront fees are hooks.

Originator: No, we don't charge non-refundable upfront fees. When would you like to get together in person and talk about your application and file?

This is a near perfect scenario. If I heard this from an Originator, this would be where I would go.

With that said, let me bring up something very important. You do not want to submit multiple applications for two reasons. The most important, even though you will be told otherwise, is that it can lower your credit score. There is no definite on this. Sometimes it does. Sometimes it doesn't. The credit repositories suggest that it doesn't but I have seen otherwise. Second, the reason you don't want to do this is because it wastes your time.   With each application, you will be submitting the documentation. This is an ounce-of-prevention versus the pound-of-cure idea.   Invest the time necessary to find the right company so that you don't have to repeat action steps.

If I heard this, would I stop making the ten phone calls? No, I wouldn't. I would make my notes on the Mortgage Company Query sheet and then call the next one. Perhaps you'll end up with three possible good companies and have a choice to make. Keep in mind that anything said about rates tells you nothing. The rate is determined by the rate sheet on the day you are ready to lock your rate. You can ask, when you are interviewing mortgage companies, if they will show you the rate sheet when you're ready to lock in your rate. If they say yes, that's a home run. It is, however, not a fair expectation.

Once you are face-to-face with the Originator, with all the support and verification documents in hand, then it is time to make some very serious points.

Client: I want to make sure that we are on the same page. Buying a house for me is the biggest investment I'll ever make.   A difference of even an 1/8 point means a lower payment and considerably less money paid over the life of the loan. So, I want you to know now that once the HUD is ready for my review, I will be looking it over. If the HUD shows something other than what we agree to, I'll stop the closing. I have already told the real estate company and the seller about this. I'm not trying to strong arm you. Rather, I want us to keep each other honest. I have all the documentation you want with me and will update both the paycheck stubs and bank statements if needed.

Another suggestion I'm going to offer is to copy your completed 1003 and extra word document pages onto a USB flash drive.   Depending on the software the mortgage company uses, it's possible the 1003 can be imported so you don't have to fill it out again. **Again, never email a completed 1003.**

From my experience, I am going to recommend that you be prepared to hear things like, "We're not the company for you," or "I'm sorry – we're professionals and don't like being treated like children," or "How we are compensated and how we run our business are not your concern," or "I'm not interested in working with you – thanks anyway." What is more important is that you don't want to work with these companies. They are giving you very clear indications that they are not committed to transparency, accountability, and integrity. A mortgage is a huge investment. For that reason, it pays to remember that **it's your money**.

Between the application phase and the rate lock phase, you may communicate with the Processor. She will only call if she needs something updated or if there is some oddball thing the Underwriter wants that hasn't been anticipated. Does it happen? Yes.

To ask, when you are locking your rate, "How much back-end commission are you earning with this rate?" is a fair question since there is an agreement that you have a say in how the compensation is paid. Other questions that are appropriate at that point include: 1) So what is your total percentage then? 2) What if I want to put all of that in upfront fees rather than back end? 3) So, you are earning 2.3% on my mortgage – what if I want to move more of that to the front and reduce our rate?

And, of course, everything is negotiable. As an example, let's say you are being offered a rate of 4 and 3/8th (4.375%). You are always free to ask for 4 and 1/4 (4.250%). When negotiating, I always go one step further than where I hope to end up. So, I would ask for 4 and 1/8 (4.125%) hoping to end up at 4 and 1/4. This will decrease the commission to the mortgage company. However, that 1/8 point will make a difference to your monthly payment.

To follow up with a question of, "And that's what I'll see on the HUD?" is also fair. Of course, these things happen at the end of the process, not the beginning.

Locking Your Rate

Knowing when to lock your rate is also one of the keys to saving money. When is the best time to lock the rate? To answer this question, I need to explain how locking a rate works, as well as penalties for expired locks. The short answer is: The best time to lock a rate is after you have a "clear to close" from the Underwriter. With that, you can request a 15-day lock.

Locks come in increments of 15 days – 15, 30, 45, 60 days and even more. However, when you execute a 30 day lock or greater, you are gambling with the Lender's money so the commission to the Broker takes a reduction ("hit") which means the Broker is going to up the rate to you to make up the difference. And the hit to the Broker, and resulting increase in your Note Rate, worsens with 45 and 60 day locks.

As mentioned elsewhere, you have hit a home run when you're working with an Originator who will show you the rate sheet. Home runs are rare in baseball and in mortgage lending as well. The one point that is worth remembering is that the compensation paid to the mortgage company is a direct result of increasing your Note Rate – that's where the commission money comes from. The cost to you, for the commission paid to the mortgage company, over the life of the loan can be five to ten times what it would have cost if paid up front.

What is a par rate? A par rate earns the mortgage company nothing. The commission is 0.00% to 0.25% at most. Can you request a par rate? Of course, provided you are willing to compensate the mortgage company in front end fees. The par rate is not, however, the lowest possible rate you can get. Your Note Rate could go lower still.

To get below the par rate, you have to understand that the mortgage company gets penalized for going lower than the par rate point. The amount of the penalty is based on the loan amount multiplied by the percentage of "below par penalty." However, if you are willing to come up with that, in addition to the front end costs, your Note Rate could go even lower yet. If you have the funds available to cover these, it is worth asking the Originator or mortgage company about this option.

If the lock expires, in other words it takes more than 15 days to get to closing, the result is, usually, that you will receive the greater of the rate that you locked or a comparable rate for that day. This is the best reason of all to wait for the "clear to close" before locking your rate.

Does it ever pay to borrow money to pay the fees upfront? With a purchase or construction-to-permanent program, this will not be possible since the money for the down payment and closing/settlement costs must be seasoned.   With a refinance, however, you can use borrowed funds to cover closing (mortgage) costs. Think of it this way: Which would you prefer to do? Pay off the closing costs in three to five years (from a personal loan) or over the course of 30 years in higher payments and interest?

Another alternative, and this works for purchase mortgage programs, is to reduce the down payment to save on payments and interest by paying the mortgage company's fees upfront. The loan amount will increase. The Loan-to-Value ratio will increase. However, it might pay for itself in the long term.

This book has one objective only – to help you save money. To do that, we sometimes have to be a little creative and a little analytical. Figuring out how to save the most money takes time and effort. Finding your best solutions can and will pay off in the end. It is worth it when you realize that the overall savings run into the tens of thousands of dollars.

CHAPTER 13: THE DISCLOSURES

The Real Estate Settlement Procedures Act of 1974 (RESPA) was enacted with the best of intentions – to protect homebuyers and mortgage loan borrowers. It has had some success. The law, however, can only do so much. People who lack integrity will always do their best to find ways around the law.

One of the major targets of RESPA was kick-backs where a mortgage loan originator pays a real estate agent for a referral, or where a title company pays a mortgage company for a referral. Those who do not respect that law will find ways around the law – usually with cash. Of course, if caught, the penalties are very severe – loss of license and fines of up to $10,000.

You might be saying, "How does that affect me?" Where do you think the money for the kick-back is coming from? You and your pocket book. You don't honestly believe that the mortgage company would pay out of their pocket, do you? No, they'll tack on a fee to cover the kick-back. Of course, you can finance that into your mortgage and pay for it over the course of 30 years.

In terms of disclosures, there are the "three day disclosures" and others. A mortgage company must provide three disclosures to you within three business days after you have submitted an application. The disclosures are: the Good Faith Estimate, the Affiliated Business Arrangements disclosures, and the Servicing Disclosure Statement.

Before getting into the three day disclosures, I want to point out that the most important disclosure of all is the HUD-1 Settlement Statement which must be available for you to review 24 hours in advance of the closing. The Truth-in-Lending Disclosure (the "TIL") is also important but not as important as the HUD. The TIL explains how much interest you are paying over the life of the loan. The HUD discloses the fees you are paying to obtain the mortgage and who receives the money. This is the disclosure that will keep a mortgage company honest. That is the intention of the HUD. However, if you don't know how to read it or what the sections mean, then the HUD can't help you and won't keep the mortgage company honest.

The Good Faith Estimate

The goal of the Good Faith Estimate is to provide an estimate of how much it will cost you to obtain your mortgage. However, it is not a binding agreement. At this point, there are many unknowns. A rate can be estimated but that is all because actual rates won't be available until your loan application is into underwriting and has been reviewed by an Underwriter.

As a suggestion, you might tell the Originator that you want him to put the mortgage company's entire fee on the front end so that you can have a par rate on the back end. This does two very important things for you. First, assuming the Originator is being honest with you, it tells you how much the mortgage company intends to earn on your mortgage. Second, without any doubt, you have just declared yourself to be an educated buyer because only educated buyers know terms like "par rate" and "back end." If you get a response of, "Well we can't do that," then you need to walk, because the company intends to exceed the 3% on the front rule. It is also an indication that you will hear "par rate" but never see the rate sheet and the HUD will disclose that there was back-end commission.

In the Loan Officer chapter, I mentioned that the first company I worked for was owned by a friend. Prior to going to work for L, my wife and I wanted to refinance our home in order to obtain a better rate and lower payment. L offered to help us refinance our home at no cost out of friendship. Of course, we would have to pay the Application Fee but he wouldn't charge us for processing or an origination fee. True to his word, he did not charge us an origination fee. We didn't understand that the application fee went in his pocket. We reviewed the HUD after the closing. L earned a 1 and $3/8^{th}$ (1.375%) yield spread premium/commission on our "no cost" loan. That 1.375% yield spread premium increased our Note Rate by at least 0.250% and probably closer to 0.500%. The point of this is to show that L is a pretty typical mortgage broker.

Let me go through the GFE section by section. You can obtain a sample GFE by searching online for "Good Faith Estimate sample" and a sample is included in the documentation package available through my website, www.PatMazor.com.

The first section provides information about the Originator and the mortgage company, you, and the date the GFE is being generated. Under "Purpose," it says this is an estimate of your settlement (closing) charges (costs) and the terms of the loan. As well, you should receive a copy of the HUD (Housing and Urban Development) Special Information Booklet.

The Important Dates section is meaningless to you. An interest rate cannot be determined until your loan package has been reviewed by an Underwriter. This is also true for any deadline on the validity of closing costs, and how far in advance you must lock your rate. The "rate lock period," item (3) is also open until you lock and set the lock period: 15 days, 30 days, etc.

Summary of your loan.

By now, you have enough knowledge about the process to know your loan amount and term (number of years). However, since you don't know what "hits" will be imposed by the Underwriter, you can't know the rate. Once you do know the rate, however, you'll be able to estimate your monthly payment and mortgage insurance charges. The first three Yes/No check boxes should all be checked "No." As of this writing, early 2013, this would be a bad time to apply for anything other than a fixed rate because rates are at their absolute lowest in decades. Very few mortgage loans have prepayment penalties. If you are opting for a 15 year term using a 30 year payment structure, there will be a balloon payment at the end of the 15 years.

Escrow Account Information provides an estimate of the monthly insurance and property tax charges. Your program may allow you to pay your own insurance and property taxes in which case the "No" box would be checked. However, there is usually a hit to doing that. As to whether your escrow account will cover all the charges, in most cases, it will.

Summary of Settlement Charges is your first opportunity to see what you are being charged by the mortgage company in Item A. Item B would include title fees, the appraisal, credit report, and other fees that are not part of what the mortgage company will earn on your loan.

Understanding Your Estimate Settlement Charges is intended to give you a very clear idea of how much and in what ways you are paying the mortgage company. Line 1 is the total estimate of what the mortgage company is charging you to broker this loan. Section 2. Although it isn't called Yield Spread Premium or Commission, this is where it is detailed. The first check box would be an indication that you are only paying upfront fees. The second check box shows you the rate that mortgage company intends to obtain for you and the amount of money that saves you in upfront fees. Now, it is time to ask a question, "How much does paying this way increase the Note Rate and my monthly payment?" Once that has been answered, then you can ask, "So, if I pay that amount, your back-end commission, upfront, that will reduce my Note Rate to **% and my monthly payment to $** which over the course of 30 years saves me $**. Is that correct?" Think about this for a second. Do you realize that most borrowers never ask about this? And, yet, it is the most critical piece of information in the entire GFE. The third checkbox is for buying down your rate even further. When I talked about locking the rate, I mentioned the option of paying the mortgage company in order to take the rate below a par rate. I believe that is what the third checkbox is for. A is the total origination charge less the commission which is the upfront costs.

Item 3 will include the Credit Report fee, and possibly the processing fee.

Item 4 is the title company's fees that you will be responsible for. In a purchase, the majority of these fees are paid by the seller. In a refinance, you.

Item 5 is title insurance – seller on a purchase, you on a refinance.

Item 6 will include the appraisal. Keep in mind that the mortgage company requests the appraisal. Again, since the mortgage company owns the appraisal, offer to meet the appraiser when he comes out to inspect the home and to pay him yourself so that, if you change mortgage companies, hopefully, the appraiser will reassign the appraisal to the new mortgage company so that you don't have to pay for two appraisals.

Item 7 is for recording the title with the city or county government.

Item 8 is for any charges related to state, county, or city fees that are not property tax related.

Item 9 is the estimate of reserves that will begin to fund your escrow account.

Item 10 is daily interest charges. These cannot be calculated properly for a number of reasons. First, you don't know your Note Rate. Second, you don't know how many days there will be between the closing and your first payment. However, this does estimate the daily payment if the Note Rate is accurate.

As to Item 11, you have already contacted your insurance company and know the name of the insurer and how much your annual premium should be. That information goes here.

B is all the items that are not involved in the origination of your mortgage loan. Add B to A (from above) and you have an estimate of the amount of money (plus your down payment) that you will have to bring to closing.

Now, let's look at Page 3. The Instructions echo the explanation I gave and the intention is clear – to let Borrowers know they have choices in how they wish to pay the mortgage company. I would be interested to know how many Originators complete the "tradeoff table" properly. The explanation is clear. This is the area to review to help you determine how much you want to pay upfront and how much you want to pay on the back end recognizing that you will be paying for those charges on the back end for the life of the loan. Perhaps it is only $20 per month. Over the course of 30 years, that is $7,200.

Using the shopping chart has its risks. Whether your credit scores will suffer from multiple applications and credit report pulls is an unknown. It is best to choose a mortgage company with comparative shopping and providing the Mortgage

Summary before your credit report is pulled rather than after. This section echoes the Mortgage Company Review document except that there are no ratings for professionalism. If the professionalism is there, the right numbers will be there.

Once again, looking at the last part of the GFE: the loan is not sold, only the servicing of the loan is sold.

Affiliated Business Arrangement Disclosure

The mortgage company will probably provide this, showing that it does not have any such relationships. The purpose to this disclosure is to let you, the Borrower, know that you do not have to use services recommended by the mortgage company and that the relationship exists. To find this online, search for "Appendix D to Part 3500." To explain that for you, this disclosure is outlined in RESPA, Part 3500, Appendix D.

Servicing Disclosure Statement

You can find this by searching for "servicing disclosure statement sample pdf." The purpose of this disclosure is to estimate the likelihood that the servicing on your mortgage loan will be sold to another lender. If you are dealing with a mortgage company (broker), obviously they will not be servicing your loan.

The TIL or TILA (Truth-in-Lending Act) Disclosure

The most interesting part of the revised TIL Disclosure is that the second page is the old form of the Good Faith Estimate. Finding a sample TIL can be a challenge. Mostly, the search identifies websites that discuss the TIL and the regulations behind it but do not provide a sample to review. Try searching for "TIL disclosure sample pdf."

The top four boxes identify the Annual Percentage Rate (APR), the finance charges (interest) associated with your mortgage loan, the amount being financed (the principal), and the total of payments – principal plus interest.

The next lines explain that your down payment (the required deposit) is not considered in calculating the APR and the "payment schedule" refers to monthly (usually) but it can be bi-monthly or even annually under some programs.

Number of payments will probably be 360 (30 years), the amount of payments will be the principal, interest, and mortgage insurance (P/I plus MI). When payments are due is the day of the month. There are three sets of boxes to cover for combination loans.

Demand Feature refers to whether your mortgage loan can be "called" or "accelerated." Simply put, if you default, the Lender has the option to call the entire loan by accelerating (speeding up) the payments. Variable Rate Feature refers to variable or adjustable rate mortgages.

Credit Life/Credit Disability is something you may wish to consider. In essence, this is life and disability insurance. Talk to your insurance agent first, however, since you may find that he has a program that will be more cost effective. You will be required to obtain homeowner's (property) insurance and, in some areas, flood insurance. The Credit Life/Credit Disability is an option.

The Security is the property itself. Filing fees were covered in the GFE. A Late Charge will be assessed if you are more than ** days late, and the percentage of that late charge will be **%.

Seldom is there a Prepayment Penalty. This section of the TIL Disclosure identifies if there is. Likewise, assumable mortgage loans are pretty much a thing of the past.

And you will acknowledge receiving a copy of this disclosure.

The HUD-1 Settlement Statement

This is the most important disclosure of all. Again, it will be available for your review 24 hours in advance of closing. I strongly recommend that you call the title company once you have locked your rate and set a closing date and ask the title officer for a time to come in and review the HUD as soon as it's available. The GFE was an estimate. The HUD will tell you exactly what the mortgage company is being paid and you can put the two documents side-by-side to see if what has been represented is accurate.

The HUD begins with a description of your mortgage loan: Type, the Title Company's File Number, The Lender's Loan Number, and the Mortgage Insurance Case (Policy) Number. Look at "C." Note: This form is furnished to give you a statement of actual settlement (closing) costs. Amounts paid to and by the settlement agent (title company) are shown. Items marked "(p.o.c.)" were paid outside the closing; they are shown here for informational purposes and are not included in the totals. The key words are "actual settlements costs."

Items D through H detail you, the seller, the Lender, the property, the title company and its address, and the closing date and disbursement date. The disbursement date is the date that the funds from the Lender will be available to pay off the previous mortgage on the property, to pay commissions to the mortgage company and real estate agent, to pay the title company its fees, and to pay the seller.

Section J, Items 100 through 303 cover the buyer/borrower's side of the transaction. The Contract Sales Price is the price of the home. Personal property would be for, as an example, appliances included in the sale. 103-Settlement Charges to Borrower comes from your down payment and closing costs. Items 104 and 105 will be additional items if any. Items 106 through 112 will be tax related items. Item 120 is the cost of the home plus your closing costs plus tax related items. Item

201 is your earnest money. Item 202 is the mortgage loan (which is credited toward what you owe at closing). Item 203 is for any existing loans, i.e., in a refinance application. 205 is a Lender Reimbursement Credit which may apply in some cases. 206 through 209 are for additional items related to what is paid on your behalf or credited to you. Items 210 through 219 are for adjustments of items paid by the Seller, i.e., property taxes to date. Line 220 is the sum of all the 200 Series (credited) items.

Line 301 is, usually, the cost of the home plus your closing costs. 302 is the mortgage loan and other credits. 301 minus 302 is how much you are expected to bring to closing.

Section K itemizes the Seller's side of the transaction. Item 401 is the contract price for the home. 402 is personal property, appliances as an example included in the sale, 403 through 405 are other items that might have been included in the transaction. 406 through 412 are adjustments for credits to the seller related to the sale and taxes. Item 420 is then the amount due the seller from the sale plus any adjustments. Section 500 (Items 501 through 519) list the Seller related obligations that are being paid off in the transaction which includes the Seller's mortgage(s). Line 520 is the amount of money to pay off Seller-related obligations. Item 601 is the total amount due the Seller. Item 602 is the reductions. Item 603 is how much the Seller is receiving in the end.

Now we get into the truly important information. Section 700 details the commissions from the sale of the property which should be 6% divided equally between the Seller's real estate representative and your representative. Any fees that are in addition to the commission will be detailed on Line 704 – perhaps a listing fee for the Seller.

Section 800 details exactly what the mortgage company is charging you for brokering your mortgage. Item 801 should be the origination (front end) fee with the percentage identified.

Item 802 is for money you are paying to reduce your Note Rate. 803 is the commission (called "adjusted origination charges"). Items 804 through 814 are other things, i.e., the Appraisal (for which, again, you will want to pay the appraiser directly), Credit Report fee, and other things. If you paid an application fee at the beginning, that may show up here as POC – paid outside of closing.

This is the section of the HUD where you will discover whether the agreements you made with the mortgage company have been honored or not. If they have, you are in great shape. If they haven't, you have choices. In the sample HUD that I provide, the loan amount is $240,285.00. The loan origination fee was $2,402.85 (1.00%) and the amount earned from back-end commission ("adjusted origination charges") is $2,402.85 (1.00%) – a total fee of 2.00% between the two going to the mortgage company.

Section 900 includes those items to be paid in advance which includes the daily interest charges for the days between the date of the closing and the first payment date (Item 901), the Mortgage Insurance Premium (902), payments due on the homeowner's insurance (903), flood insurance and property taxes (905) which may be paid by the seller. In essence, Section 900 gets things caught up to the closing date.

Section 1000 goes into the reserves/prepaids to fund the escrow account to cover for property taxes, homeowner's insurance, mortgage insurance, or flood insurance. 1001 details your total initial deposit. 1002 through 1006 breaks down that total deposit into the various categories and any aggregate adjustment (credit toward the prepaids).

Section 1100 covers the title-related fees including the title insurance premium (1101), the settlement/closing fee charged by the title company (1102), the title search fee (1103), Lender's title insurance policy (1104), and limit declarations in terms of coverage for the Lender and Borrower (1105-1106). Items 1107 through 1111 are title company and state specific.

Section 1200 covers the government-based recording and other fees. Section 1300 details any additional charges and Line 1400 provides the totals owed by both the Buyer/Borrower and Seller.

The last page of the HUD draws a very clear comparison between the Good Faith Estimate provided to the Lender and Title Company and the actual charges. The question is, then, is the Good Faith Estimate that you received from the Originator the same GFE? And, finally, the bottom half of page 3 of the HUD restates the TIL disclosure.

It is important, when you review the HUD prior to closing, to take the Good Faith Estimate given to you by the Originator with you and make side by side comparisons with it and the final page of the HUD. It is also a good idea to look at the top section of page 3 carefully with regard to the mortgage company's compensation. Is this what you agreed to with the company?

Most important of all, remember that *it's your money* that is buying the house, paying for the house, and paying most of the fees related to buying the house. *It's your money,* meaning that you have an opportunity to have a say in the rules.

What if the numbers aren't what you agreed to? The best thing to do is to ask for a copy of the HUD, go to the mortgage company in person, and then restate the agreement that you had providing the Originator with his GFE and the HUD. You may hear something along the lines of, "I'm sorry – there's nothing I can do to help you now." That is not true. You could answer, "Very well. As I mentioned at the beginning, if the HUD does not reflect our agreement, I will stop the closing and that's what I'm going to do. I discussed this with the seller and real estate agent in the beginning. You have two choices – and you will have to cover the draw documents fee, I'm not covering that – you can either re-do this so that it meets our original agreement or we'll go find another mortgage company. As was the case with you, we have all the documents we need for processing. So, it's up to you. What do you want to do?"

It is my hope that this won't happen. If it does, you're prepared and know what steps to take. Again, *it's your money*.

CHAPTER 14: SUMMARY

Mortgage Rip-Offs is meant to be educational and to help you understand the industry and how it works. Sadly, the majority of mortgage companies are not what you are looking for. Not too long ago, as an example, I was looking over a couple of the mortgage groups on LinkedIn and saw a post that literally floored me. One of the members asked the following: "Do any of you know of a Lender who is offering a SISA program? We really need those." I covered SIVA and SISA programs in the chapter on mortgage types. SIVA stands for Stated Income-Verified Assets. SISA stands for Stated Income-Stated Assets. It was the SISA programs that had a lot to do with the foreclosure crisis. Borrowers state their income – no verification. And, they state their assets – no verification. But they have good credit scores. It's not enough. A SIVA program is great for someone who is self-employed and writes off most of his income to save on taxes. There will be verifiable assets. Assets indicate substance and net worth. This assumes mid-scores above 750. Stated-Stated indicates nothing at all no matter how good the scores are.

SISA programs are the natural alternative for people who are buying more house than they can afford.

I hope you enjoyed *Mortgage Rip-Offs*. I hope you have come away with a better sense of how the system works and what you can do to save money. Please feel free to email questions or comments. My email address is Pat@PatMazor.com. Thanks for reading *Mortgage Rip-Offs.*

Made in the USA
Middletown, DE
08 March 2015